Some Shropshire Gardens

Barbara and Alan Palmer

Shropshire Books

Front Cover: Parsons Pleasure, Acton Burnell
Back Cover: The Dairy House, Ludstone

ISBN 0-903802-45-7   © Text Barbara Palmer   © Photographs Alan Palmer 1990
Cover and book design: Sarah Barker
Editing: Helen Sample
Published by Shropshire Books, Shropshire Leisure Services, Preston Street, Shrewsbury
Typeset by Litho Link Ltd, Welshpool, Powys, Wales
Printed in Great Britain by Printex Press Ltd

Contents

Foreword

The first Shropshire garden of note I ever visited was that of John Treasure at Burford House, Tenbury. That was twenty years ago and I was a newcomer to what was then one of the most underrated of English counties. Some years later I came to know Pat and the late Mike Edwards whose garden Swallow Hayes at Albrighton is a mecca for plantspeople. It is through this friendship that I became involved in the annual and highly successful Shropshire Gardens Competition which is run jointly by Roses and Shrubs of Albrighton and the Shropshire Star.

Over the last seven years in my capacity as a judge I have travelled the length and breadth of the county visiting gardens of all shapes and sizes and of all persuasions. Each year I have seen gardens entering the Competition for the first time, some old and occasionally newly rescued from oblivion, others recently made and already impressive. In writing and illustrating this book Barbara and Alan Palmer have provided the ideal guide for those countless enthusiasts who, like myself, pursue the joys of garden exploration from the first snowdrop to the last autumn leaf. It is a fascinating selection from the manor house acres with their arboretums to the humble cottage gardens with their echoes of the Victorians. Many are open to the public at some time in the year and having visited several of them myself I can promise the reader a rare old time.

Roy Lancaster

Gatacre Park, Bridgnorth.

Introduction

It is easier to state what this book is not, rather than what it is. It is certainly not a guide book, nor yet a catalogue of the plants found in the fifty-eight gardens visited. I suppose the best description is a celebration of gardens in Shropshire, or two highly personal opinions in words and pictures of an incredibly varied garden scene.

Inevitably some gardens were preferred to others, strong preferences, even prejudices, dictate that this is so; but all the gardens were valid statements reflecting someone's ideal landscape. In fact it was extraordinary sometimes how the creator's personality was mirrored in their garden. One almost knew what the owner would be like after seeing the plot.

Shropshire is one of the largest and least populous of the lowland English Shire counties, and, in spite of the new town of Telford in the east of the county, this still holds true today. The overall impression is of a gently rolling agricultural county, in parts reminiscent of a by-gone age, whose passing is long regretted further south and east: real countryside, instead of that semi-agricultural half urban sprawl or intensively farmed treeless desert that now covers so much of the Home Counties and the East Midlands.

Geologically Shropshire is unbelievable diverse. Rocks from ten of the twelve geological periods are found within the confines of its long border. The Wrekin is ancient palaeozoic, Wenlock Edge composed of the Silurian limestone so beloved of fossil hunters and the flat lands close to the Herefordshire border and round Bridgnorth, pure Old Red Sandstone. It naturally follows therefore, that its gardens should be equally varied. Although we travelled over two thousand miles and took seven hundred pictures in a period of eight months, it was never difficult to discover a new angle, or find a fresh topic at each of the gardens visited. The weather was on our side of course, though the early season and the hot sun forcing plants into full bloom and over their best in a few days, contributed to the sense of urgency.

We found the exposure to so many gardening experiences crystallized our ideas about what we liked and disliked. Meticulous over-planned gardens definitely losing out in our estimation to a more natural country-garden approach.

Peoples' reasons for indulging in gardening were also fascinating. Some owners were pure collectors, less interested in garden design than in ensuring they had every form of a particular species. Others were intent on creating a perfect landscape in miniature, or satisfying a human need to be close to nature, perhaps as a contrast to their working life. Some treated their gardens as pure therapy, just another hobby to put life into perspective. Yet more withdrew into their gardens, reflecting an urge to be in a different world, like reading a book or listening to a piece of music.

We could not, of course, have produced this book without the co-operation of the garden owners, who gave so generously of their time to take us on conducted tours of their domains, plied us with cups of coffee and patiently answered endless questions –

our grateful thanks to them all. A very special thankyou to Sarah Stafford, who I am sure saved me from many botanical errors.

Finally, the book has given us an opportunity to acquire a first-hand acquaintance with Shropshire gardens, which we shall always remember, and to explore parts of the county which were completely unfamiliar to us. The point driven home again and again is that everything in Shropshire is on such a delightfully human scale. There are mountains, but not too high, many lakes, but none too large, small copses, not trackless forests and superb country houses. We are fortunate indeed to live in such a beautiful place.

Alan and Barbara Palmer

A wisteria, planted 1917, clothes the walls at Ashford Manor.

Ashford Manor 🌸 near Ludlow

A medium sized natural garden, with an emphasis on good foliage for flower arranging. Open under the National Gardens Scheme, see Yellow Book.

The house and garden at Ashford Manor have a strange history. The present owner, who has been in occupation since 1928, decided to sell the too large house and grounds when he inherited them. As this proved impossible, he engaged a good architect and proceeded to reduce the house by nearly a half. He has lived in the house now for over sixty years, so I hardly need say that he did not regret the decision.

Looking at pictures of the house and garden before the renovation, it is hard to believe they are the same. The house was a typical Victorian stucco building with a formal garden bordered along one side by a magnificent serpentine wall. The same wall today is the only clue that you are looking at the same property.

The top storey of the house was removed, it was reduced on the south side by a further amount, and, best of all, when the stucco was taken away, mellow, grey-fawn sandstone in excellent condition was revealed.

The garden was transformed from the formal to complete informality – a totally natural garden in keeping with the metamorphosis of the house. The basic idea behind the remaking of the garden was an emphasis on good foliage for flower arrangement, in which branch of the Arts the owner was professionally involved (he is also an excellent watercolour artist). There is an all pervading feeling of the past around Ashford Manor and garden. One absorbs a sense of the late Victorian Arts and Crafts movement. William Morris might have lived in the house and been inspired by the garden when creating his fabric designs; especially the strong foliage shapes of cardoon, aquilegia and yucca.

The house is surrounded by a dry stone terrace made of the same material. There are broad steps facing west and south, and the entire walls, steps and paving play host, indeed seem held together by, a myriad of self-sown flowers. Especially valerian, pink and white, eryngium, the sea holly, lavender, ballota, hawkweed, sage, thymes in variety and many more, all growing in happy disarray. Good shrubs give a firm base: *Berberis* 'Rosy Glow', a fine *Juniper* 'Pfitzeriana', while a quite magnificent wisteria grows over the west front of the house. Fascinating to know the exact date it was planted – 1917.

I discussed with the owner the happy knack self-sown

Red valerian and purple sage at Ashford Manor.

plants have of putting themselves in the correct position, but decided that we probably overestimated their ability, as we both pulled up those in inconvenient places when small.

The border backing up against the serpentine wall has a more regulated air. Here flourish the cardoon, a quite fabulous form with extra deeply cut leaves, also bergenia, an unusual pink small flowered scabious, *Helleborus foetidus*, cotoneaster, euphorbia, purple fennel, white foxgloves, alchemilla and many more 'architectural' plants. The contrast in leaf form is particularly good, hard-edged round bergenia against the bronze fuzz of fennel.

Island beds house an enormous yucca dating from Victorian times, another flat juniper planted especially for cutting, and an old white cottage paeony with just one central red petal.

The owner is the third generation to inhabit the house, which was once the base for a cider making operation, the whole area behind the house being given over to a vast orchard. In fact, another great brick wall indented with filled arches was part of the factory in which the brew was made. The owner tentatively dates this building at about 1780. An aunt from whom he inherited the property was responsible for creating a natural pond as well as planting many fine trees, including some huge Wellingtonias.

The west front of the house looks over a meadow of wild flowers growing in grass; that most difficult of all garden scenes to keep looking good throughout the year. We saw it at perhaps the best time, in early June before it grew tired under hot summer conditions, when it was a mass of ox-eye daisies, buttercups, campions, and a tall hawkweed. The views beyond the meadow can only be described as stupendous: green of trees and fields merging into blue of distant hills and sky. The garden is meant to look perfectly natural. It is a tribute to the owner's skill that he has succeeded so well.

Astley Abbotts House ✸ near Bridgnorth

A black and white Tudor house in five acres of lawns, dotted with magnificent trees both native and exotic. Open under the N.G.S., see Yellow Book.

So much of the atmosphere in a garden depends on the house it surrounds and the setting, the spirit of the place. At Astley Abbotts House both are perfect.

The main house was built in 1600 and many of the large yews in the garden must be contemporary with it. Like the house, however, the garden has been added to and improved by every family who has lived there. On one side of the house spacious lawns slope down to a small hidden stream running in a deep gully overgrown with native beech trees. At the season we visited, the new growth on the copper beech glowed tawny pink against the brightness of the sky. Bridges cross the gully at several points, but no attempt has been made to construct anything other than a wild garden so far from the house. Every aspect depends for its charm on the glory of the trees and a sprinkling of blue and white bluebells in the long grass.

One only has to absorb the atmosphere in this garden for a few minutes to realise that the owners of the house are romantics. Who could fail to be otherwise living in such a setting? Huge Incense Cedars, Scots Pine, Red Cedars and Wellingtonia tower upwards at every point. Close to the house a magnificent Cedar of Lebanon sweeps the wide lawn with darkly green skirts. The owner tells of viewing the house at night in an attempt to make up their minds about purchase (it was too big, too expensive, too far from their work place). After one glance at the cedar by moonlight, they bought it anyway.

If I had to choose only one tree to transplant miraculously into my own garden, it would be the common English yew, *Taxus baccata*, which stands at a corner of the house. So often one sees yews severely clipped, when they make the most satisfactory hedges in the world, or grouped in graveyards where they jostle and push against church walls. The yew at Astley Abbott stands proudly alone without a single close neighbour, so that one can admire its untrammelled beauty from each side. I have never seen a more wonderful tree so correctly placed,

Clematis montana drapes a low stone wall at Astley Abbotts.

so absolutely right in exactly the perfect position. Everything in a garden constantly changes, even a plant which grows as slowly as the yew, but this one is at the peak of perfection, perfectly green, perfectly in keeping with its setting. Architecture, tree, sky and grass combining to give an unforgettable and very English gardening experience. I know it's a contradiction in terms, but this garden was contrived to look natural, and succeeds.

There is more formality close to the house, where a stone terrace surrounds it on two sides with steps leading down to the lawn. But romance wins out again, as purple wisteria climbs the black and white checker-board walls, and *Clematis montana* 'Grandiflora' (white) and *var. rubens* (pink) drape themselves over the mellow sandstone balustrade. Further along the terrace, large square stone planters, which look as if they might have been there when the original house was built, are packed with blue and yellow pansies.

The present owners continue the tradition of planting for the future, adding mulberry, walnut and four new Incense Cedars. The house and garden are close to the road which runs through the village, but nothing disrupts the tranquil setting, its nearest neighbours being as architecturally distinguished as itself: a part Norman church with chancel and stained glass contemporary with the house, and other black and white or sympathetically mellowed brick village houses.

Benthall Hall ❀ Broseley

A Victorian garden surrounding a late sixteenth century Tudor stone house. Benthall Hall belongs to the National Trust and is open several times a week in season.

3

The building of Benthall Hall in the late sixteenth century coincided with a sudden increase in the varieties of ornamental plants known to gardeners. At about the same time printed books on the subject also began to make their appearance; 'The Gardener's Labyrinth' by Thomas Hill probably being the best known. While the garden at Benthall Hall does owe something of its style to this Tudor revolutionizing period, more especially the great banks of lavender, box hedges, and neatly clipped standard yews, it is mainly of Victorian design, laid out and developed in the second half of the nineteenth century.

There is evidence of a visit by William Robinson who admired the many plants cultivated, especially the crocus collected in Turkey, Europe, and North America by George Maw, who lived in the house at the time. The large rockery to the west of the house was laid out by another tenant, Robert Bateman and his wife. This part of the garden has some good trees, which are now so large that the rockery no longer functions as such. It is a maze of narrow rocky paths, the borders between tightly packed with ferns, pulmonaria, hellebores, hypericum and acanthus. There is another layer of shrubs-skimmia, roses, and berberis, overhung by trees-prunus, acer, magnolia, sumach and ornamental cherries. All these are packed in like peas in a pod, jostling and pushing for position. I liked it. It was far more original than an ordinary rockery.

To begin at the entrance to the garden, one walks in under what must be one of the largest beech trees in the country. It towers overhead, its already considerable height emphasised by the fact that it grows on a bank. The tiny church which sits on the periphery of the garden, was once a private chapel for the Hall, reminding one of the religious upheaval going on when the house was built. The family were Catholics, hence the remains of priest holes found in the house.

Topiary on stilts, an Elizabethan concept in the largely Victorian garden at Benthall Hall.

The great sandstone house, with its beautiful mullioned bay windows and star-shaped chimneystacks, dominates the garden, which falls into two distinct parts: the rockery and terrace on the west side and the section close to the house which retains its open character, with a formal oblong pool, small beds of roses underplanted with *Viola cornuta*, delightful standard clipped box and yew topiary on stilts.

One walks upwards to a sundial and another long narrow pond. Dianthus in all shades of pink and red contrast beautifully with the grey stone. Paths are cobbled and overhung with neat humps and tuffets of gorse, heather, tanacetum and dwarf hebe.

The dovecote at Benthall.

Further up, where the terrace begins to be overshadowed by the rockery trees, grow Russian sage, santolina, and herbacious paeonias. On the dovecote wall (inhabited by a slumbering white dove at the window) are *Paeonia suffruticosa*, the Chinese Tree Paeony, in pink and white.

The front of the house faces south before a square of grass with rounded edges set in gravel, and is completely different. The eye travels over a sloping lawn and a ha ha into a classic English landscape. It was good to see the new planting of blue Atlas Cedars, which will be magnificent when mature. Fully grown trees frame this view, mostly oaks, yew and Bay Laurel. Under the trees grows a wonderful dark purple hardy geranium, *G. psilostemon*, a native of woods in Turkey. It has a dramatic black eye and glows in the dim light.

The sloping lawn has banks of juniper, hypericum, ferns, epimediums, acanthus and hardy geraniums, matted together in a most successful ground cover. The acanthus seem to be winning the battle, but who cares? With such fabulous leaves one can never have too much of it.

A side lawn houses a most delightful thatched rustic summerhouse, set under the shade of some large limes. Close by I noted *Picea pungen glauca*, the blue spruce, and *Cornus mas* 'Variegata', usually seen in the unvariegated form.

Geranium psilostemon *at Benthall.*

Formality reigns as one moves closer to the house. Two beautiful wide urns grace the top lawn. They have four faces carved in relief, with swags in their mouths, and are planted up with the small pansy 'Jackanapes'. An unusal but inspired choice as it is contemporary with the house.

Finally, the narrow border under the high walls of the house contains several fine climbers including a wisteria playing host to a white *Clematis montana*, a *Clematis alpina* and, I think, *C.* 'Little Nell' – white with a mauve edge, also a dark red rose, perfect against the grey stone. Lower plantings are of hardy fuchsia, sedum, *Anemone japonica*, hydrangea, paeony and self-sown poppy. The latter were all in yellow, though the orange form of *Meconopsis cambrica* is much commoner. They looked well against the blue creeping campanula, *C. garganica*.

This is a relatively small intimate garden, not at all what one expects round a great country house, but none the less charming for that. Benthall is not elaborately landscaped, nor (with the exception of the crocus) does it have a vast collection of rare plants, but the domination of the great sandstone house, with its long historical associations, make a visit to the gardens a nostalgic experience for any true romantic.

Breidden Way ✿ Bayston Hill

A small suburban garden, which is an object lesson in both design and maintenance. Not open to the public.

It is a sad fact that most keen gardeners do not have a large plot in beautiful surroundings to develop. The majority are faced with the regulation 25 × 100 feet strip at the rear of the house and a pocket handkerchief in the front, together with a typical 1950 or 1960 semi. Often there are main roads, awkwardly placed telegraph poles, other houses and maybe a garage or ugly commercial buildings to contend with as well. Occupants of this type of garden seem either to sink without trace, opting for a square of more or less green lawn, narrow borders and a regulation couple of daffodils, or rise magnificently over the disadvantages.

The garden at Breidden Way falls very definitely into the latter category. The tiny front garden is a glorious example of carpet bedding at its very best. Each plant superbly grown, the colours well thought out from the yellow-green edging of *Pyrethrum aureum* 'Golden Moss' to the pink and white single begonias, so close not a pencil could be slipped between them. Above rise standard fuchsia giving a further band of colour, the centre piece a striking twelve year old example of 'Voltaire'.

The owner states that he never gets frustrated with his small plot, because the form of gardening he has chosen is so intensive. All his time is fully occupied growing as many as seven thousand plants, to say nothing of their careful planting and maintenance with all that implies in watering alone. The whole lot are changed in the autumn for a winter/spring scheme based on Universal Pansies and polyanthus. The aim is the simple one of continual flowering without a break all summer.

Because of the limitations on space, the car has been banished from the drive, which is given over entirely to tubs and pots overflowing with geraniums, petunias and yet more fuchsias. Hanging baskets on the house wall hold trailing lobelia, nasturtium and ivy leaf geraniums. I greatly admired the standard lantanas, which I first mistook for verbena (they are the same family). The round bunches of tiny flowerlets change colour as they mature, from cream to peach to pink, in the most delightful way, contrasting well with the rough green leaves.

The back garden (120 × 24 feet) is a triumph of design over difficulty. The aim here was to disguise the edges and cut the length visually. This has been most successfully achieved by a curving pattern and the careful use of conifers. Although there was plenty flowering in this part of the garden, the overall impression was of restful green.

Everything is in perfect taste, as well as being meticulously planned never to be out of scale within the restricted space. A well made open sided summerhouse is sited in just the right position half way up the garden. I loved the Russian Vine, *Polygonum baldschuanicum*, growing over it. It has to be clipped twice a year, and therefore never flowers, but was an unusual and effective roof. The owner constructed the summerhouse, paving and edging himself to fit the garden, as he despaired of finding anything suitable on sale.

The same attention to detail is evident in the building of the two raised ponds, each surrounded by greenery, including some fine examples of the prostrate juniper, 'Blue Star'.

The back garden was planned on paper eleven years ago, only two trees being retained from the original conception. It looks surprisingly mature, probably because the owner was able to commandeer several large specimen shrubs from a relation's garden. Also acquired in this way was a large terracotta urn planted with the variegated *Euonymus fortunei radicans* 'Variegatus'. This is a trailing

Carpet bedding par excellence, Breidden Way.

form with green and white leaves, sometimes tinged pink, also good for wall or ground cover.

Various growing conditions have been deliberately created to suit different plants. There is a scree of gravel for low growing alpines, and a green island bed, planted for spring with rhododendrons. Conifers, variegated ivy and heathers make lovely foliage contrasts later, and give the eye a rest from the more colourful parts of the garden.

There is a tiny fenced patch with a circular lawn, planted with *Chrysanthemum multicaule*, a long lasting yellow buttercup-like flower, which looks wonderful, and stands up well to hard wear.

The rear garden is almost entirely surrounded by tall, clipped, conifers *(Chamaecyparis lawsoniana)* which give shelter from wind. All the conifers, both in and around the plot, looked in excellent condition considering the hot summer which encourages red spider mite. The owner has to spray to eradicate this pest, although he doesn't like using chemicals.

There are two alpine troughs, again restfully planted in green, and an arch of *Clematis montana var. rubens* leads into the working area. Here a large frame with a removable plastic top holds the winter bedding, while three greenhouses burst with fuchsia cuttings and spare summer bedding. Not an inch of space is wasted. This garden is obviously lived in and loved, providing beauty, therapy, interest and a creative outlet all the year round.

Brimstry ✽ Albrighton

Over two acres of well laid out trees and shrubs, some rare and all interesting. Open under the N.G.S., see Yellow Book.

Brimstry can best be described as a small arboretum rather than a garden. It consists of a large area of undulating lawn, sloping gently down from a low modern bungalow. The garden is dominated by five magnificent giants-an oak, horse chestnut, lime *(Tilia × europaea)* and two copper beech. The owner was heart broken when one of the beech lost a large portion of its upper trunk and a huge branch in a storm, but its enforced pruning exposes the smooth green-grey trunk, and does not look too out of place, though the tree has lost its symmetry.

There are beds of shrubs, including a comprehensive collection of rhododendrons, but the raison d'etre of the garden is the trees. Most, with the exception of the aforementioned giants, were planted eight or nine years ago; but the garden is still in a state of flux, with many new specimens being added every year, and a large pond planned on the site of an old orchard. I admired the owner's resolution as he constantly removes trees which get too big for their positions, enjoying them while they fit in, but rejecting with no hesitation when they outgrow their allotted space.

This type of garden, almost entirely devoted to rhododendrons and trees, is very unusual in a suburban area, but an excellent solution to the problem of what to do with a large plot if you lead a busy life. The garden always looks good at any time of the year without a programme of constant weeding, lifting and fertilizing, while all the help needed is a man to cut the grass. Some shrubs have been added in the past eighteen months, but these too are chosen with low maintenance in mind. There are plans to include a few more herbaceous perennials, other than the single island bed already in existence.

The sorbus caught my eye when we first entered the garden, with their superb display of berries. Some were

Early autumn at Brimstry.

used to back a large rhododendron and azalea bed, while *S. hupehensis* and *cashmiriana*, together with a *Ginkgo biloba*, looked wonderful against the dark glossy-green of a holly. The former sorbus has the usual pinnate foliage which colours so well in the autumn, and pink-tinged white berries. Cashmiriana has large fruit, like white marbles. Both these will come easily from seed if you remove the pith as soon as ripe, and plant in pots of sand in a cool greenhouse. They germinate in March the following year. I would also recommend *S.* 'Joseph Rock', with yellow fruit and quite outstanding autumn colour. Birds are strangely reluctant to touch the fruit.

A small area somewhat apart from the main lawn houses several beautiful, if immature, pines. *Pinus ponderosa* makes an enormous tree given time, and is one of those destined for the 'chop' when it gets too big. I don't think I would have the heart to cut it down, as the long needles, held in groups of three, are so pretty. *Pinus wallichiana*, the 'Bhutan Pine', doesn't grow quite as tall, and superficially resembles *ponderosa* when young. It has long, blue-green needles, very thick, making the urge to stroke irresistible.

I saw *Betula* 'Gold Cloud', the new yellow-leaved birch, for the first time, and although all birches are delicately pretty, I think the somewhat mottled foliage will be an acquired taste. I much preferred an older, more elegant beauty, *B. pendula* 'Purpurea', with dark plum foliage.

The owner was especially proud of a waist-high specimen of *Embothrium coccineum*, or the Chilean Fire Bush. It is very tricky to grow in Shropshire (or anywhere but the extreme South-West for that matter) and requires deep moist lime-free soil in a sheltered position, as well as some luck with your first one or two winters while it becomes established. Given the luck, it covers itself with brilliant orange-vermilion flowers in early summer. Bodnant in North Wales housed a magnificent collection before the dreadful winter of 1982, but I do not think that even they have replanted.

Prunus 'Kanzan' and *P. avium* 'Plena', both very large trees, frame the house: Kanzan a burst of pink and Plena a glorious mass of drooping double white flowers in early spring. These cherries are decidedly *not* for the small garden (my Plena is all of thirty feet and nearly as broad) but an unforgettable sight when well placed. I like the way each individual leaf turns colour in the autumn, giving a pointillisme effect similar to a Seurat painting.

I must mention a shrub – *Cotinus coggygria* 'Flame'. Its round green leaves are a pleasant change from the more usual dark red forms. All cotinus, purple and green, colour well in the autumn.

A screen of trees, mostly leylandii, protect the garden from wind, and also serve to disguise totally the fact that you are in an ordinary suburban road in a small town. The owner sees the garden as a peaceful retreat from the cares of everyday life and a place of beauty and tranquility, giving an interest out of doors divorced from his usual occupation, without being too much of an encumbrance if he wants to leave it for a few weeks or even months in the growing season. I think he has succeeded in his objective supremely well.

Broncroft Castle ❀ Tugford

A large walled garden, surrounding a perfect miniature medieval castle. Open under the N.G.S., see Yellow Book.

Broncroft Castle is a garden of walls. Not a walled garden precisely, but a plot full to overflowing with outbuildings large and small. Never have I seen such a beautiful background utilized so well. Not an inch of space is wasted, the old sandstone muted to a mellow red-gold by the years playing host to roses, honeysuckle, clematis and more unusual climbers, as well as providing a sheltered haven for a myriad of other tender shrubs and perennials.

The house is the nucleus of this garden. Built originally in 1382 by Sir Simon Burley on the site of a previous Norman castle, it has been significantly altered over the years, but still retains the air of a fortified manor house. A sense of history pervades the whole area. I was not surprised to learn that it had been held by the Royalists in the Civil War, then taken by the Parliamentarians who used it as a jail! It was partially demolished at this time but later rebuilt, first in the time of Charles the second, and later in 1840, when

Medieval castle walls at Broncroft, a perfect backdrop for roses, wisteria and creeping plants.

most of the outbuildings were constructed. The whole hangs together so sympathetically it is hard to believe it was not all built at the same time. This is probably because old stone from the site has been used and re-used constantly through the ages.

All garden designs tend to be variations on a few basic themes, their diversity coming from the plant material used. Broncroft follows the pattern of wide lawns bordered by herbaceous beds close to the house, leading into a wilder more natural garden with shaded river walk further from the main buildings. The delightfully clear River Tug runs in a sheltered valley near the eastern flank of the house. This part of the garden is a wonderful wilder contrast to the more formal areas. I loved the tiny stone-edged island, complete with weeping willow, in the centre of the river, and the beautiful azaleas and rhododendron, their strident colours muted by all the surrounding greenery. Close to the river a bank thickly planted with hosta and Solomon's Seal leads right down to the water, again a lovely contrast to the bright hues.

Also in this wilder portion are self-sown Sprengeri tulips, glowing bright red, lighting up the gloom under the trees. There are alliums and euphorbia as well, all responsible for putting themselves in place.

There are many good trees in the garden. As well as our native beech oak and alder, I noted *Ginkgo biloba*, several forms of crataegus and a eucalyptus in a sheltered corner.

Everything is perfectly in tune with the house. There was not a jarring note, from the cobbles left untouched (never mind that they are difficult to walk on) to the careful use of outside lighting. I keep becoming diverted from the garden back to the house, but must mention the beautiful and curious twisted chimneys, which are visible from many parts of the garden and provide a backdrop to the trees.

The beds close to the walls blend the wild and the formal, paeonia and wall-flowers interspersed with self-sown *Meconopsis cambrica*, the wild Welsh poppy in orange and lemon. A happy idea, as paeonia are here today gone tomorrow, while wallflowers and poppies go on forever.

The vegetable garden is worth a chapter alone. It is roughly triangular in shape, backed on two sides by a low wall and separated from the main garden by a wonderful undulating yew hedge. Many of the vegetables are grown in raised beds. I think this an excellent idea, as it facilitates picking and pest control and one can retain complete control over the soil content. This part of the garden also has a delightful long border full of the older cottage-garden flowers and herbs-alchemilla, tansy, nepeta, aquilegia, orange blossom and yet more paeonia. Soft fruit has a border to itself, again backed by a sandstone wall. There is a

The wild garden at Broncroft.

11

perfect summerhouse at the apex of the triangle and a sundial in the centre of the garden to give a vertical element as a focal point. The good firm structure is an object lesson in how to lay out a formal kitchen garden.

Moving closer to the house, the changing nature of the garden is emphasised by a pretty wrought-iron gate at one side of the vegetable plot and tall yew piers on the other. Walking through the latter, one again has a view of the house and wide lawn which dominate the more formal area.

The stone wall separating the garden from the lane is hung with native wall plants, valerian and larkspur. It backs a well thought out shrub border, as good in foliage as flower, with dark red *Cotinus coggygria* in the form 'Royal Purple', spiraeas and viburnums.

Finally, I must mention that though many owners have contributed to the gardens, for twenty-five years they have been in the care of Mr. Tom Lloyd.

Brownhill House ❀ Ruyton XI Towns

A medium sized garden clinging to one side of a river valley. Open under the N.G.S., see Yellow Book.

There are enormous advantages when gardening on a very steep slope, but, as the occupants of Brownhill House have discovered, these are counterbalanced by an equal number of disadvantages. Amongst the latter, the one and a half acre garden faces north-west with all that implies in cold winds and lack of direct sunlight. The advantages encompass free-draining sandy loam and a beautiful position in a totally rural valley, with a pleasant river at the bottom of the steep hill. The owners of the garden added unlimited enthusiasm and a grim determination to tame the wilderness they found of deserted scrap-yard, nettles, brambles and dead trees when they acquired the property in 1972.

As they worked in very difficult conditions without help, it was inevitable that the garden should take shape over a long period, influenced largely by ideas picked up on garden visits, reinterpreted in their own way. The owners estimate that it took thirteen years to complete the outline – and it isn't finished yet! I noticed a half completed sandstone folly, standing stone and Celtic cross, as well as a small scale laburnum walk, inspired by the great laburnum tunnel at Bodnant.

At the top of the steep slope, which encompasses almost the only large flat area in the whole garden, is a beautifully laid out and tended vegetable garden. This was where the owners began so many years ago, working down the slope directly opposite, then across to the far boundary of the river. They terraced as they went, building steps and paths, planting each reclaimed area with a medley of bulbs, shrubs and trees.

There are no great rarities or exotics, but all the plant material is well chosen to suit its position and the limitations of the site.

I particularly admired the gunnera, rheum and tall pink spiraea, doing so well near to the river bank. It is so much better to go with your garden, to take advantage of its natural assets, than strive to grow something alien to its micro-climate. The river provides an inexhaustible supply of moisture, so why not take advantage of it? This river (The Perry) which adds so much to the atmosphere in the garden, fortunately does not flood, though the Local Authorities have dug out the bed in a somewhat unsympathetic manner to facilitate the flow of water. It will be some years I fear before the banks are once again well clothed in foliage.

The moisture loving plants on the Brownhill House side were not touched however, and have now reached an impressive size and spread. These architectural plants need space all around to show to the best advantage. They look quite superb against the river valley landscape behind, and with an expanse of rough grass in front.

The river walk at Brownhill House is delightfully in keeping with the wilder parts of the garden, even the sprinkling of buttercups on the opposite bank of the river adding to the composite picture.

The difficult terrain at Brownhill House.

In fact, my overall impression is of a great range of gardening ideas in a small space, without that 'crammed' feeling that one so often gets. Variety is the keynote, from the formality of the vegetable garden and the terrace, to the wilder semi-woodland area further away from the house.

This is of course, by its very nature, a labour intensive garden, but the lay-out and size mean that even uncultivated almost vertical banks given over to completely natural ground cover of ivy or Enchanter's Nightshade somehow knit into the garden picture without any loss of continuity. The garden is full of the self-confidence the owners brought to what must have seemed a daunting proposition.

Brynhyfryd ❀ near Oswestry

An acre of heather, alpines and conifers on a wild Welsh hillside. Not open to the public, but specialist nursery alongside open at the weekends.

Some gardens blend in with their surroundings, others stand out. Brynhyfryd falls very definitely into the latter category. It occupies an acre of east facing borderland hillside (half of the garden is in Shropshire and half in Wales) and was created out of a bare expanse of nettles and docks.

The garden grows three types of plants superbly; conifers, heathers and alpines, as the neutral (pH6.5) well drained gravelly clay is perfect for all of them. Surprisingly, dwarf rhododendron and supposedly acid loving heathers also flourish, proving yet again that both these plants are a good deal more adaptable than was once realised.

The owners have lived in the low grey stone house for seventeen years, building up the garden slowly from single specimens, seed and the odd cutting. Very little was bought in.

A green raoulia clothes rocks, Brynhyfryd.

The collection of conifers is quite outstanding. I saw the garden ten years ago when they were still young, but they have now matured into multi-coloured multi-textured sentinels, providing height and interest above the great patches of carpeting heathers. The owners make a point of planting all the heathers in large blocks, and it certainly adds to the impact. I also noted *Euryops evansii*, with its delightful blunt-tipped silver leaves, growing en masse, when the grey colour shows to greater effect.

There is very little definition between the garden and the mountain. Sheep graze right to the edge of the simple wire fences, while more heather, gorse and sheep scattered hills press in all around. Goldfinches and ravens breed in the surrounding countryside, while stoats and rabbits invade the garden.

Precipitous rocky paths wind up to the house at the top of the slope. There are several large ponds which are in the process of being renovated, and which add yet another facet to the garden. The top of the garden close to the house is home for most of the alpines, and it would be difficult to imagine a better natural habitat. We didn't see them at the correct time, planning our visit to look at the heather garden, but many were still in flower. Some are rare, all are interesting, and the owner obviously knows and loves each one individually.

One which stood out for me was a raoulia, which looks exactly like green moss flowing over the rocky outcrop it inhabits like a thick velvety river. Most of these minute leaved plants from Australia or New Zealand are silvery and require perfect drainage for success. Once established though, they are perfectly hardy. *Oenothera lutea* is an extraordinary and rare form of the Evening Primrose. It looks not unlike a dandelion but without the toothed leaves. A fascinating characteristic – a flower bud opens visibly at about half past three every day, and is over by evening. The owner states that if you turn your head, you often miss the show so quickly does it happen! I was also intrigued by a large prostrate silver-leaved plant which comes from the Falkland Islands. The metallic, rounded leaves are not unlike those of a bergenia – which the plant also resembles in habit of growth – though it is in fact a senecio, it is believed *S. uliginosa*. Only recently introduced, I am sure it will be a future favourite among all plant connoisseurs who value beauty of leaf as much as showy flowers.

Alpine shrubs include the aforementioned dwarf rhododendron and an excellent collection of daphnes. These include all the old favourites such as retusa, cneorum, and blagayana as well as temperamental beauties like tangutica and collina.

There are so many beautiful conifers, it is once again almost impossible to pick out just a few. In any case, a great deal of their interest comes from the subtle contrast in colour, shape, and leaf texture. They are certainly better in carefully considered groups, than dotted individually about a garden. There are many *Juniperus communis* 'Compressa', a perfect miniature Noah's Ark conifer; *the* one to choose when planning a trough garden. The owner has a rare gold form which has just appeared and will be propagated in time. I also admired *Picea albertiana* 'Conica', a fluffy leaved bright-green perfectly shaped cone.

The heathers suffered badly during a bitter February a few years ago, when the east facing garden took the brunt of a fierce wind. Many were not replanted, though enough remain to give spectacular blocks of colour throughout the year, including the depths of winter. The owner's only maintenance in the established beds, apart from pulling out an occasional perennial weed or foxglove, is to clip over the lings once a year after flowering.

The many troughs of alpines are another feature of the garden well worth a visit on their own. They are carefully grouped in natural stone containers, as interesting out of flower with their colourful congested foliage as when in full bloom.

Brynhyfryd is also famous for the many lewisias grown, both species and hybrids, some raised on the premises. The majority are grown in pots, but are bone hardy in the open. Some tips which I gleaned to aid cultivation are that they do not *have* to be planted on their sides, but enjoy good drainage; also to place egg-sized stones round the crown (plant slightly above the soil) which enables the wind to blow through and dry out the base of the leaves. All lewisias are gross feeders in pot or garden and can produce hundreds of flower spikes if given enough to eat. Most come from the Rocky Mountains in North America and actually enjoy a cold winter. Damp is their enemy, together with impoverished soil.

This is a unique garden, both in situation and planting, which by careful choice of plants derives the maximum potential from a most unpromising position.

Burford House Garden ❀ Tenbury Wells

Four acres of superb gardens designed by the owner in 1954 and set in unrivalled surroundings on the River Teme. Garden open daily in the spring and summer, nursery open all year, but restricted opening during the winter months.

Burford House was one of the first gardens I visited early on in my gardening evolution and therefore holds a special place in my affections as it helped to formulate my thoughts on the ideal garden.

It is not a very large garden in the style of Bodnant or Powys. First impressions are somewhat deceptive, as the lines of the garden lead the eye on and the outer limit is mostly hidden by trees.

The red brick house which gives the garden its name was built in the eighteenth century when formality was the keynote in garden design, but, except for the long pool on the north side of the house, the garden owes much of its charm to the irregular island beds planted with perennials in varying heights, a distinctly *modern* concept in garden planning. The beds are superbly planted with many unusual shrubs and herbaceous perennials, several of the taller bushes acting as hosts for the extensive collection of clematis for which the garden is famous (Burford House holds the National Collection of Clematis, many of which are obtainable in the nursery attached to the garden).

It was at Burford House that I first realised a clematis did not *have* to be trained on a trellis against a flat wall, usually exhibiting a long stem of unattractive wood without either a leaf or flower, the latter growing in an untidy bunch at the top. At Burford some one hundred and fifty clematis scramble through species roses, cling precariously to other climbing plants growing in the conventional way on warm red brick walls, and weave themselves in joyous abandon through a bed of heathers. Until one has actually seen an almost completely prostrate clematis, you can be quite unaware of the charmingly natural picture it can present.

It is impossible to name even a small percentage of the clematis, but look out in particular for the rarer species, such as *Clematis montana* 'Picton's Variety', an almost red form of the common pink or white, at its best in May. The named varieties of alpina and tangutica are so superior to the forms grown from seed, such as 'Francis Rivis' in the former and 'Ludlow and Sherriff' or 'Bill Mackensie' in the latter. Also the real rarities which one only ever has the opportunity of seeing in the flesh, so to speak, at a clematis specialist. Examples might be – *Clematis florida* 'Sieboldii', the Passion Flower Clematis, which surrounds its central boss of purple stamens with a frill of greeny-white outer petals; even rarer, its cousin *Clematis florida* 'Alba Plena', all

Meconopsis inhabit a favourite position in damp shade at Burford House Garden.

greeny-white, as if viewed through still water.

Not surprisingly for Shropshire, the gardens are in a frost hollow, but the variety of plant material is immense, with walls and mature trees offering some protection.

I mentioned earlier that the garden lies close to the River Teme, but this river runs in a hollow and is not visible from most of the garden. Two smaller streams have been created however, which are fed with water from the main river, providing the inexhaustible supply of water so necessary for a successful moisture garden.

Beautiful, carefully thought out plant associations abound throughout the garden, but I found the moisture garden with its wonderful collection of hosta and candelabra primula particularly satisfying.

Close to the water, but not actually in it, can be found quite the best specimens of veratrums I have ever seen. This excellent foliage plant is always tricky to place – moist shade, no slugs, just the right amount

Superb colour combinations, Burford.

of light – but how magnificent it is when well grown, each rich green leaf a perfect origami fan pleat, followed by tapering spikes of dark-purple flowers. The variety *V. album* has white flowers and *V. viride* grey-green. Flower arranging exhibitions are sometimes held in the house. In the stable block is a small museum which tells the story of the garden and also contains pictures portraying the genus Clematis.

Children bored by garden visiting will find the ornamental ducks on the 'Old Moat' close to the car park a welcome relief from plants.

Chyknell ✸ Claverley

A formal garden designed by Russell Page surrounding a classic Regency house. Open under the N.G.S., see Yellow Book.

Some gardens are of special interest because of their association with great gardeners. Such is Chyknell, designed in 1950 by Russell Page.

Page was a garden designer active from about 1930 to the late 1950's. He was an original thinker and a true artist in every sense of the word; an international gardener influenced as much by French and Italian garden tradition as English. His book, 'The Education of a Gardener', is one of the great garden classics, bringing his ideas before a wider audience, and not to be missed by any serious garden designer.

Not all of Russell Page's ideas survive at Chyknell; lilacs he planted, for example, have died out, but enough remains to appreciate his general theme.

17

The house, built in 1812, simple and elegantly Regency in form, sits squarely in a typical rural landscape of farmland, distant low hills and superb trees. Each side of the house faces a widely divergent outlook, all pulled together by the rural surroundings. The front of the house, dignified by a colonnaded entrance, faces north-east. This unpromising aspect looks out over a flat lawn bisected by the wide entrance path and seven magnificent yews. The spirit of the place here breathes Druids and ancient mysteries.

The owner has no knowledge of a previous building on the site, though the stables date from about 1792, but the yews must be a great deal older than the present house.

Walking round the house to the left of the entrance one comes to the first of Page's designs, a semi-enclosed oblong of shaved yews (neatly tying into the frontal aspect) approached downwards by shallow steps, the stone dogs at the top, echoed by doubles clipped out of the living hedges. The eye is drawn over the square formal pond to an unobstructed view of far away Claverley church tower, shimmering in a blue heat haze. Very little colour here, but none is required, the structured architectural bones of the garden, the medley

Russell Page's pleached limes at Chyknell.

of greens fading to blue are all the distraction required.

The rear of the house is a typical Russell Page tour de force. A formal lawn is bordered by a pleached hedge of lime trees, backed once again by clipped yew, a wonderful dark contrast to the spring-green of the limes. A parallel border, also with straight stiff hedges and ending in a wrought iron gate, lies to the left. It was once filled by roses, carefully graded by Page in size and colour, from dwarf to standard, palest pink to deepest red. The sandy soil did not suit, however, and herbaceous perennials now fill the wide borders.

A delightful courtyard, the paving stones interplanted with alpine and creeping plants, is sheltered by the projecting wings of the house. A mature *Magnolia grandiflora* on the wall overlooking the courtyard had been badly frosted in spite of the protection and favourable south westerly aspect, but ceanothus, wisteria and the tender *Rosa banksiae* 'Lutea' flowered undamaged.

A rosemary, also in full bloom, sprawled over the stones at their feet, surely the only way to grow this notoriously difficult to place shrub.

The western side of the house offers the complete contrast of a woodland walk with gravel, bluebell-strewn paths and flowers spilling over from the grass borders. Here the emphasis is all on the natural, a perfect break with the formality close to the house.

One cannot help wondering, walking around the garden today, what Russell Page would have thought of it. I think he would have been more than delighted with its mature beauty.

The Dairy House ❀ Ludstone

A large three acre garden, planned around an old quarry in a beautiful village setting. Open under the N.G.S., see Yellow Book.

Friends had exhorted me many times, that I *must* go and see The Dairy House, that it really was special, my kind of garden. I can only say that having got there at last, I was not disappointed.

The situation is perfect. The Dairy House sits comfortably in the middle of an old sandstone hamlet, that looks as if it has been forgotten by the modern world. On one side is the beautiful Jacobean manor house of Ludstone, with an ornamental lake making up another boundary to the garden. The rest of the property consists of an old quarry, which provides a natural amphitheatre and focal point in the centre of the garden. So much of a garden's charm depends on its surroundings and, at The Dairy House, they couldn't be bettered. One sees the facade of Ludstone Hall from the

sloping lawn at the rear of the house, forming an impressive backdrop to the plants. The lake (I believe it was once part of the moat that surrounded Ludstone Hall) is a mixed blessing. Facing east, it funnels cold winds into the garden and holds the frost in bad winters, while looking serenely beautiful under a July sun.

The first indication that The Dairy House was indeed as special as I had heard was the sight of a whole long border against a stone wall devoted to that most difficult and yet desirable perennial, *Romneya coulteri*. Like an extra large white poppy, with petals of finest tissue paper centred on a boss of golden stamens, if you grow this plant well in your garden, you have definitely arrived in gardening terms. Fiendishly difficult to propagate, and therefore almost impossible to obtain, your troubles are not yet over, as it hates disturbance and sulks at first. Once it does get going, however, it often perversely takes over the border, as it has at The Dairy House.

The border which holds the Romneya continues towards the house in a medley of blue and white interspersed with grey. White scabious is set against nepeta and

Hypericum calycinum, *The Dairy House.*

19

lavender, with ceanothus contributing its own cerulean tinge against the wall. The grey note comes from mounds of helichrysum. Further up the slope, tuffets of the dwarf *Campanula carpatica* were a mass of pale blue and white blooms. This is a much underrated plant for the front of the border. It is best grown hard in poor soil – even gravel – when it makes a neater clump, and can be raised from seed.

The pea-shaped pinky-mauve flowers of an indigofera caught my eye in the main border. I had always thought that they were somewhat tender, but the gardener (who has been there over twenty-four years) assured me they were not. Nearby grows the grass, *Elymus arenarius*, with steely-blue leaves and a graceful habit of growth. A favourite plant of Gertrude Jekyll, it apparently has immense flower spikes later in the season, but is to be treated with caution, as it is *very* invasive.

At the top of the sloping lawn one turns left to skirt the old quarry, looking down into a large grassed hollow, laid out with immense island beds. The sides of the quarry are planted up with ground cover both shrubby and herbaceous, while the left hand side sports a magnificent holly hedge grown entirely from self-sown seedlings dug up in the garden – what a wonderful and practical idea. The gardener stated that he simply added another length every year as he found more plants.

Ground cover used on the steep sides of the quarry included *Hypericum calycinum* (St. John's Wort), vinca, viburnum, phlomis, sumach, syringa (lilac) and shrub roses. The scent was delicious. Everything is natural with nothing out of place. The steps which bisected the bank and led downwards halfway along are constructed of simple free-draining gravel, held in place by rustic logs.

A large *Buddleia alternifolia* marked the top of the steps. This had been well trained on one stem to make a delightful weeping small tree. You have to be ruthless with this buddleia, which flowers incidently on the *old* wood and must not be pruned in spring. Do not let it make a mass of suckers. It has sweet smelling bunches of small mauve flowers, set along its arching branches.

Apple trees with twisted trunks add to the old-world air in this part of the garden. The whole area was originally designed by a Mr. Percy Cane, who came back about ten years ago shortly before his death, and must have been delighted with the way his plans had matured. He had a few somewhat grandiose ideas (such as a temple in what is now a wild part of the garden) but this was wisely resisted by the owner.

The large island beds on the floor of the quarry, contain some very interesting plants. One consists mainly of heathers and conifers, but I noticed a delightful magnolia in full flower. This was the rarely seen *M. 'Watsonii'*, with small upward facing white flowers, set off by dark red centres. It has a very strong scent like so many of the magnolias. I also admired the pollarded *Paulownia tomentosa*, with extra large leaves. These are of course enlarged even more by the pollarding treatment. Many trees with large or interesting leaves can be cut to the ground or severely pruned in early spring, enhancing their size and shape. The elder, *Sambucus racemosa* 'Plumosa Aurea', and the sumachs, *Rhus glabra* and *R. typhina*, in their cut leaf forms, 'Laciniata' are particularly responsive to this treatment.

Close to the house is a long bed set against a hedge, containing a colourful mixture of orange and yellows. These hues were supplied by huge groups of Day Lilies (hemerocallis), Evening Primrose (oenothera), and Red Hot Pokers (kniphofia). Shrubs included a superb yellow berberis, and the aforementioned Cut Leaf Elder. The garden in fact contains a tremendous variety of Day Lilies. They make large trouble-free clumps of grassy foliage which resist weed penetration and need no staking. Day Lilies are also disease free, and are now available in many new colours, though the old-fashioned orange shades of *H.* 'Kwanso Flore Pleno', and the bright yellow of *H.* 'Golden Chimes' are hard to beat. The large trumpet-shaped flowers last only one day – hence the name

– but more are produced on a regular basis.

One memory to carry away – a cherry trained on the wall of a rustic building, covered in fruit. No flower could have been prettier than the bunches of ripe fruit set against the old brick wall.

David Austin Roses ✾ Albrighton

One of the most comprehensive collections of roses in the country. Open all year with the exception of Christmas Day, Boxing Day and New Year's Day.

David Austin Roses is first and foremost a commercial nursery devoted chiefly to the raising, cultivation and sale of what are generally known as 'Shrub Roses'. To the rear of the commercial beds and sales area however, Mr. Austin has planted out what must be one of the largest and best collections of these roses in the country.

Climbing rose 'Bobby James'.

It encompasses all the many sections: First old roses – Gallicas, Damasks, Albas, Centifolias, Moss Roses, Chinas, Portlands, Bourbons and Hybrid Perpetuals: Then the true shrub roses – Rugosas, Hybrid Musks, Modern Shrub Roses and Ground Cover Roses: Rose species, including their hybrids: Climbing Roses, Rambling Roses, Hybrid Teas, Old Hybrid Teas and Floribundas: Even small roses – Patio, Miniatures and Dwarf Polyanthus. In a new separate circular garden grow a David Austin speciality, the English Rose. These are described by Mr. Austin as, 'New roses in the old tradition'. That is, they have all the qualities of fragrance, variety of flower shape and soft colour which have stimulated interest in the Old Shrub Roses, without their greatest fault of only flowering once a year.

There is no doubt that if you want to see roses, whether with a view to buying for your own garden, or just for the sheer pleasure of being overwhelmed by a glorious heady mixture of sight and scent, a visit to this garden in late June or July will literally take your breath away.

It is inevitable that the serried rows of roses out in the flat fields and the surrounding commercial buildings detract from the atmosphere. It is after all, as much a catalogue as a garden. But great efforts have been made to isolate the garden by planting surrounding shelter belts of neatly clipped *Cupressus leylandii*. (Very necessary I should think on the flat windy plain which borders the nursery.)

In the rose garden well-built piers of brick support rough-hewn wooden arches which add height and interest as well as supporting the many climbing roses. The central aisles are beautifully paved in brick, while a group of statuary placed at the end of this vista gives a focal point. Another piece provides a centre for the circular garden of English Roses.

How can one make a selection from such a vast and comprehensive collection, either to plant in one's own garden, or describe in detail? Choosing roses is a very personal activity. I have known gardening friends who are at one on practically every other horticultural topic, almost come to blows over roses (usually the eternal Hybrid Tea and Floribunda versus the Shrub Rose argument). To make matters worse, the older, and to me most desirable, roses are fair sized plants and can even be described in some cases, such as *R. moyesii*, as small trees, very much at odds with the size of the modern garden.

Rosa 'Ferdinand Pichard'.

A smaller garden needs to go for good value. For example, one glorious flowering for a week in June may be alright in a couple of acres, but is of little use in a pocket handkerchief, when one must sit and look at the admittedly not very exciting foliage, or thorny twigs, for the other fifty-one. There are two ways of tackling the problem. In a large garden I like to grow the roses on their own in a separate bed, with perhaps just a little low ground cover. Even if you are very fortunate in the size of your plot they are best grown in an enclosed garden where high walls or hedges capture and intensify the scent, then hide the unprepossessing remains for the rest of the year. Alternatively, in a small garden, one can incorporate the roses into a mixed border, and, if they are large and quickly over, use them as a prop for a climber. This need not necessarily be a clematis, though many are admittedly excellent, but could be *Eccremocarpus scaber* for example – quick and easy with orange tubular flowers.

There is only one massed planting at David Austin Roses, this is just as you come in round the car park. It knocks you out with a wave of pink, while helping to hide the admittedly unprepossessing buildings. In the rose garden, there are necessarily only single specimens or small groups. I can only pick out some personal favourites which looked good at the time of visiting.

If I only had one rose, it would have to be the *gallica* 'Rosa Mundi', the perfect striped rose in crimson and white. This one is not too big and can be pruned. Madame Hardy, a damask rose, would come a close second. This has exquisitely shaped white flowers, with a tiny green centre. It is scented, and makes six feet in my garden. I have just acquired Queen of Denmark, one of the very best of the shrub roses. It has big pink flowers and healthy foliage. I must mention William Lobb, which is a large gaunt moss rose, dark crimson at first, but fading to an unusual mauvey grey. This makes a good support for a climber. The rugosas Blanc Double de Coubert and Roseraie de l'Hay are unbeatable in a poor position, or on dry sandy soil. They are both big, but do flower later in the year and have bright yellow foliage in the autumn. A really tiny rose for the small garden is Little White Pet. It has small white pom-pom flowers and blooms over a long period. I couldn't imagine a garden without *R. xanthina* 'Canary Bird', with arching branches covered in fern-like foliage smothered in bright yellow single flowers. This grew magnificently for me on sandy soil, but I have reason to believe it is tricky on heavier ground and must not be pruned, when it can suffer from die-back. Cecile

Brunner is the most exquisite miniature rose, with perfect little pale pink blooms. Get the climbing form, which is very vigorous, up to twenty feet. Finally, *Rosa banksiae* 'Lutea', a very vigorous thornless climber, which *must* have a warm wall, when it will produce Victorian posies of tiny double, pale yellow flowers on the old wood.

Dingle Bank ✿ Chelmarsh Common

A one acre garden, containing an impressive collection of herbaceous perennials. Open under the N.G.S., see Yellow Book.

Many people carry a vision of a dream cottage at the back of their minds – low, white, nestling in a hollow, close to a stream and sited in beautiful unspoilt countryside – all to be acquired at some future date. The owners of Dingle Bank found their cottage twelve years ago, then proceeded to create a dream garden around it.

The previous owners ideal was to live in the middle of a wood, and to this end, he planted the ground with a thick mixture of birch, larch and conifers. The new owners'

High summer in the herbaceous borders at Dingle Bank.

first task, after completely redesigning the interior of the house, was to cut down most of the trees and get to grips with the acre or so of garden, though a nucleus of trees was retained.

The garden was so colourful when we visited in late July, one might be forgiven for thinking that it is a one season garden, at its best in high summer. This is far from the truth however. Bulbs brighten spring, early shrubs continue the show, shrub roses herald mid-summer and the vast variety of herbacious perennials take over in June and July, bringing the display to a triumphant conclusion. The shrubs provide further late autumn colour from leaf and berry, to make it a truly all year round garden.

The basic design, which was completed a little at a time, consists of island beds with mown grass between. They vary in size, some planted in one sitting, when a colour and texture plan was used, others gradually built up over a long period, when plants were added as acquired.

The variety of plants used is tremendous. Phlox in particular are special favourites, and I noted every shade, through white, pinks, reds, mauves and the variegated. Both of the best forms of the latter are represented, 'Norah Leigh' with a great deal of cream on the foliage and pale lilac flowers, and 'Harlequin' with less variegation and darker purple blooms. 'Norah Leigh' is the preferred form, being more vigorous and prettier. Phlox often suffer from eel worm, which ruin the plants, so take care to buy from a reliable source, and be careful when accepting a clump 'over the fence'. They also dislike hot dry positions in poor soil.

Close by was the lovely pale cream anthemis 'E.C. Buxton', though the form grown at Dingle Bank was purchased as *Mrs* E.C. Buxton, and appears to be noticeably taller.

The soil in the garden is heavy, which suits most of the perennials very well. It is a labour intensive garden, with many beds to edge (over a dozen island beds alone). The owner states that she enjoys the edging and weeding however, finding it therapeutic after a long day indoors. The surroundings are certainly beautiful, the quiet and tranquility conducive to peace of mind.

A small brook runs at the bottom of the garden in a deep shady ditch. It dries up in mid-summer, but the base remains damp, and the soil is extra good, giving a place to grow moisture loving plants such as primula and mimulus. The owners had main sewerage put in last year, which necessitated digging up this area. They found the experience somewhat traumatic, but used it as an opportunity to rearrange the plants into a more satisfactory design.

The garden is rather cold and windy, though the steepish slope means that there is no frost hollow. The surrounding high hedges and rough woodland cut the wind from all corners but the west, where there is an open view over the Shropshire hills. I cannot believe that it is *so* cold however, as the brilliant red *Lobelia cardinalis*, in several forms, grows well and survives the winter on a regular basis.

The owner has an unashamed love of colour, and makes no effort to restrict her range to the soft muted 'cottagey' shades. She feels a garden needs the vibrant jazzy tones, and uses them to great effect all over the place.

There are no ornaments in the garden, but steps constructed of gravel and pinned logs, good paths and low raised beds of sandstone give the garden substance. Conifers in a variety of shapes, colours and foliage also create interest when leaves of deciduous trees have fallen. There are few annuals, but I noticed good old *Papaver* 'Pink Chiffon', which looks like a congested ball of petals, and always seeds true in my garden, and at Dingle Bank. The very occasional single flower is as pretty as the double.

At the far side of the garden is a circular lawn approached through an arch, with a wide border surrounding (a good contrast to the circular beds of flowers in grass). Agapanthus in various forms, not just the popular extra hardy Headborne Hybrids, looked superb, also a stokesia, which has a blue cornflower-like bloom and evergreen leaves. I find it somewhat tricky in my garden, and have never succeeded with it for long, but at Dingle Bank it looked very healthy. I suspect it has enjoyed the recent hot summer and mild winters. Another plant I find difficult to keep, but which does well here, is *Salvia officinalis* 'Tricolor', a sage variegated in pink green and cream. The purple, green and cream, and the common green form are a great deal easier to grow, if not quite as pretty. General advice is to try three plants, three times (if you can afford it) before you give up for ever. I would also add – try them in widely different parts of the garden. Its amazing how often the one in the *worst* position survives!

There are over thirty shrub roses in the garden, and a vast variety of other plants, but for me the herbaceous perennials are the real glory. It would be hard to find a finer collection, so well grown, anywhere.

Dudmaston ❀ near Bridgnorth

A classic English combination of grass, trees and water. Dudmaston is owned by the National Trust and opens frequently in season.

Dudmaston is superbly sited on a south facing slope, overlooking the Clee Hills and a large lake. The grounds were landscaped in 1777 by William Eames, who was also responsible for work at Erddig and Chirk Castle. He specialised in the then fashionable practice of converting or extending rivers and boggy ponds into vast sheets of ornamental water. The whole impression at Dudmaston is of wide open, spacious park land, with judiciously placed trees and sky-reflecting water.

Two magnificent Cedars of Lebanon at the side of the great house make interesting tiered sculptural shapes, echoing an owner's obsession with this branch of the arts. Both inside and outside the house are many modern pieces by Barbara Hepworth, Henry Moore and others. The outdoor sculpture sits beautifully in the uncluttered, green landscape, the light reflected from the water, or the sculpture's own image mirrored below, adding an extra dimension.

Of greater interest to me than the parkland surrounding the house, is the wooded valley known as the Dingle. A small stream which feeds the main lake flows through it. This small picturesque wood was laid out in the middle of the nineteenth century in the best romantic traditions, with urns, rustic seats and arbours, many dedicated with flowery Victorian inscriptions to

Metasequoia glyptostroboides.

friends and relations. Every effort was made to help nature along by damming the river to create cascades, plotting winding paths through the trees and constructing mysterious recesses for seats. Everything in short to produce the Victorian ideal of a small scale romantic landscape of the type idealised in Pre-Raphaelite paintings of a slightly later date.

The creator of the Dingle was a gardener named Walter Wood, who imbibed his ideas from an even earlier romantic garden made at the Leasowes, Halesowen in the mid-eighteenth century. This area is now being restored to its original glory and should contribute much to the gardens at Dudmaston. A perfect Victorian Gothic landscape in miniature, it is one of the very few examples of this style of landscape gardening in the country.

Extensive rhododendron and azalea plantings in what was known as the American border were severely damaged in the great frosts of 1982. They are being replanted, but one does not go to Dudmaston primarily to look at the plants, rather to absorb the unique atmosphere, revel in the rural landscape and admire the fine trees. Geoffrey Wolryche Whitmore, 1908-1969, was an active manager of the estate and brought in an enlightened forestry practice which is now bearing dividends.

There was an attempt in the early nineteenth century to construct some formal terracing between the house and the lake. Stone steps and urns lie in the sweeping lawns, dwarfed by the sheer scale of the house and the magnificent views. Dry stone, red sandstone walls and steps in intricate patterns also lead downwards to the lake on one side of the house. This area is planted with drought-resistant helianthemums and heathers, or herbs such as lavender and thyme.

Specimen trees, as well as the mighty cedars, include one of the earliest *Metasequoia glyptostroboides* planted in the country. When we saw it in early May, it was ringed by a carpet of bluebells, a perfect contrast to the fresh green foliage.

Many ladies who resided at Dudmaston over the years developed an interest in botany, adding new plants to the garden as well as collecting and pressing those already there. This tradition has been continued in an extensive collection of work by great botanical artists of the past, as well as more modern work from the twentieth century. These paintings – exhibited in the house – and the challenging outdoor sculpture make a visit to Dudmaston a unique experience for any gardener.

Dunval Hall ✾ Bridgnorth

A medium-sized pretty garden, surrounding a superb Elizabethan black and white house. Open under the N.G.S., see Yellow Book.

The garden at Dunval Hall is distinctly modern in concept, containing both a tennis court and a swimming pool. The house it surrounds, however, is a splendid example of Tudor timber-framed architecture built in 1598. Only one portion of the garden is in keeping with the period, a delightful pair of topiary birds, who eye one another across the lawn at the front of the house.

The garden lies on three sides of the house, which sits at the top of a slope looking over wonderful views towards Brown Clee, Titterstone Clee, and – on a clear day – Caer Caradoc. The owner has gardened at Dunval Hall for forty-four years, during which time much development and extension has occurred. I admired the way the swimming pool – so alien in any garden, but especially close to a Tudor house – has a pretty landscaped sunken garden all of its own, invisible unless you hang over the wall surrounding it. The owner has treated this pool garden in an Italianate style, with stiff dark green junipers and creeper-hung sheltering walls.

A delightful white cast-iron seat fits well at the top of the pool. This was presented by the owner's father to Bridgnorth, where it was to have a permanent home outside the Quay House, close to the river in the town. When the latter was demolished, however, the owner of Dunval Hall spotted the seat and didn't hesitate to rescue it. It couldn't have a better home; in fact it might have been made for the position it now occupies. Continuing the cast-iron theme, I particularly liked the cartouche

Dunvall Hall, a perfect Elizabethan house.

set into the pool wall, which broke up the blank expanse. The pattern was echoed in the lovely cast-iron gates, made from the same old balustrade as the cartouche, and very effectively recycled, which led into the paved garden close by.

The piece de resistance here, though, was a superb marble Romanesque font, dating it is believed from about 1400. It makes the most wonderful centre piece for this small enclosed garden surrounded by high walls, the floor a mass of creeping thyme and spreading blue campanula.

A long walk, called appropriately 'The Deck', has the tennis court on one side and a long series of rough stone buildings on the other. These were once farm buildings, but are now utilized as storage, pool filter house, etc. The reroofing was undertaken by the owner, who admits to a penchant for building walls as well. The buildings provide a sheltered long wall which is planted with numerous tender shrubs. These include peaches, figs and a *Magnolia grandiflora*. At the end is a large *Vitis vinifera* 'Purpurea', the purple-leaf vine, looking especially good against the grey stone wall. The thirteen trees opposite the farm buildings are all sorbus, beautifully shaped without any pruning and not too big.

After 'The Deck', you come to 'The Bastion', a semi-circular raised area, with a new, but well-weathered, brick wall leading down to tree dotted meadowland. This part of the garden was constructed with the aid of a mechanical digger, and successfully marks off the garden from the fields. There is an excellent late flowering border for summer colour in the fallow months of August, and several good hybrid tea roses along the edges of the wall. I loved the seat placed strategically to admire the view, with a half-moon wall behind for shelter. The coping stones were again constructed by the owner, who cleverly used a mould made of an original stone.

Behind this part of the garden is a small wood with rough grass and bulbs. A good strain of semi-cultivated bluebell flourishes here, extra large in size, which make a wonderful show in the early spring.

A compact lawn at the side of the house has a yellow and white border containing that common, but much underrated plant, *Lysimachia punctata*, or loosestrife, and white daisies. The background is most unusual; a whole hedge of the Purple Hazel, *Corylus maxima* 'Purpurea', most effective.

The yellow theme is continued in a short avenue of laburnum. There is no attempt to construct a tunnel, but the whole concept works very well. The trunks have all divided, and they are not too close together to prevent appreciation of each tree individually. An interesting point; one side is *L. × watereri* 'Vossii', with extra long racemes of flowers, the other *L. alpinum*, a smaller broad-headed tree. The latter is sometimes known as Scotch Laburnum.

Having walked all round the garden we end in front of the house, which faces a wide lawn dotted with specimen trees, including a still immature cedar. The house is quite beautiful, with star-shaped brick chimneystacks and a fascinating pattern of timber lozenges. There are two projecting gabled wings, and the area in front of the door has four raised beds full of geraniums. Just the right amount of formality to complement the symmetrical house. Dunval is altogether a most interesting garden.

A final note – the owners have a house in Spain and swop plants between gardens, experimenting to find out what will survive in Shropshire.

Erway Farmhouse ✽ Dudleston

A medium sized woodland garden, packed with rare and interesting plants, now in the process of renovation. Open under the N.G.S., see Yellow Book.

Spoken of in the company of keen gardeners, the name 'Erway' brings a gleam to their eye and a knowing smile of pleasure. Long before I had ever set eyes on it, stories had reached me via the gardening grapevine of its collection of galanthus bulbs – before Erway I had thought there were just single and double snowdrops – the glory of the hellebores, forty or more distinct kinds of orientalis alone, not to mention all the later trees, shrubs and perennials. Most gardens are at their best in early summer. Erway reaches its finest moments closer to the beginning of the year, though when I visited it in June 1984, the beds in front of the house were ablaze with literally hundreds of that rarest, reddest tulip – Sprengeri. I never dreamt that in just two years the house, garden and all it contained would be mine.

Now I have had the pleasure of living with the garden for over two years, watching in disbelief the jostling dog tooth violets, *Erythronium dens-canis*, shooting up in incalculable numbers in the far border, examining on my knees the congested yellow centre of that most difficult of all snowdrops – Lady Elphinstone, and wondering over the superb *Euonymus oxyphyllus*, only ever seen before in botanic gardens.

It is not all honey of course, nothing ever is. Erway is situated on the notorious Dudleston clay belt, clay so impervious, that my neighbours claim you can throw useable pottery from it. Fortunately the ground has been worked over for many years, manure, cinders, straw, etc. being added in quantity, so that the top layers at least are amenable to cultivation. Clay also makes up for the difficulty in working it by being one of the most fertile soils to garden on.

Erway is a smallish garden (just over an acre). Most of the ground to the front and sides of the house are a light woodland planted some time ago. The numerous trees and shrubs include many rare willows, under-planted with iris, species paeonia, ferns, lilies, fritillaria, alliums and hardy cyclamen, to name just a few of the many genera represented.

The rear of the garden is more open, but sheltered by tall hedges. Of special interest here are several big speci-mens of *Abutilon vitifolium*, with vine-shaped leaves and large flowers in shades of white and mauve. They are usually only seen up to this size – about fifteen feet – on the milder west coast of the British Isles. Also in this part of the garden is the golden, upright elm – *Ulmus* × *hollandica* 'Wredei', one of the few elms resistant

Nectaroscordum siculum, Erway.

Allium giganteum en masse are a feature at Erway.

to Dutch Elm Disease. When lit up by the late evening sun, the leaves of this can produce a blaze of yellow to outshine the brightest flower in the garden.

The large square vegetable garden, also surrounded by high hedges, is in the process of being turned into a formal cottage garden (if that is not a contradiction in terms) with a deep shrub rose border and various sun-loving perennials as a contrast to the wilder woodland shady area. The aim here is profuse planting in a tightly controlled, geometric pattern of square paths and formal beds.

The roses include the wonderfully floriferous single yellow – *Rosa xanthina* 'Canary Bird', moyesii and rubrifolia, as well as numerous hybrids, all of which appreciate the rich, well-worked soil of the old vegetable garden. Growing on the walls of the house are the mature climbing roses – 'Veilchenblau', the nearest thing to a blue rose I have ever seen, a muted grey-lavender, and *Rosa banksia* 'Lutea', a somewhat tender rose that only blooms really well on a warm wall, and produces bunches of pale cream, double flowers not unlike a Victorian posy.

Plants and seeds from the garden are sometimes available when the garden is open to the public.

Farley House ❀ Much Wenlock

A one acre garden on a sloping site, containing a comprehensive collection of plants. Open under the N.G.S., see Yellow Book.

Farley House labours under a very unusual disadvantage. It is near a quarry which showers the garden with lime dust, giving a very high pH reading – over 8. This, together with the lime in the soil, restricts the plants grown to lime tolerant species. One would never guess, however, as the range on view is extensive, and, apart from the lime, the soil is excellent – a well drained, shaley limestone, overlaid with fertile clay.

When the owners moved in nine years ago, it was a wilderness of fallen and standing trees, so friable leaf mould adds to the rich mixture. The owners realized the potential in the steep site surrounded by woodland at once. Discovering a glade white with thousands of snowdrop bulbs at the top of the slope, soon made up their minds to buy.

The garden is a partnership, though the work divides into terrace building and planting. The former carried out by the male and the latter by the female half of the husband and wife team. The owners were fortunate in finding much material from demolished buildings, all of which was utilized to terrace the steep ground.

There is a quite outstanding collection of alpines, the lime haters, planted in troughs. One very original idea for growing them, is a large cement slab, raised knee high on brick pillars, and covered in sawn tufa. This 'table' is virtually slug proof, with a few pellets scattered round the base of the 'legs', and looks wonderful set in paved and terraced surrounds.

Once again, individual good plants were too numerous to list, but a few outstanding ones were a double, dwarf campanula, *C. × haylodgensis* 'Flore Pleno', very like a double *C. cochlearifolia*, which is a tiny harebell; also *Anemone palmata*, a small pale yellow anemone, easy from seed, and *Mertensia asiatica*, with blue leaves and flowers, the latter like tiny tubes.

The house is a typical, whitewashed brick cottage, about two hundred years old, which sits well at the base of the steep slope, surrounded by a large flat area of paving. The paving is cement, but has weathered so well, it looks perfectly in keeping with the house. Many pots and troughs give interest to the flat ground. There is also an island bed mulched with grit and filled with dianthus, *Allium christophii*, with huge round heads, *Eryngium bourgatii*, crocosmia, dwarf hebes and acaena. Height comes from self-sown verbascum, and a tall, variegated grass, *Spartina pectinata* 'Aureo-marginata'.

Fuschias grow to enormous size close to the house, revelling in the protection and the recent mild winters. 'Mrs. Popple' is deservedly a great favourite, with its large, red and purple flowers, but I prefer the smaller blooms and more graceful growth of *F. magellanica gracilis*. The owners of Farley House grow the variegated form, which has reverted in part, making a delightful mixture. If not cut out at some time, however, the unvariegated shoots will eventually swamp the choicer material. Also in this house bed were those great, late summer standbys *Caryopteris × clandonensis*, with aromatic leaves and pretty, bright-blue flowers, and *Perovskia atriplicifolia*, with long narrow shoots, tipped with lavender-blue flowers. It has grey leaves and whitish stems – a lovely contrast. Agapanthus in white and blue grow between to produce an outstanding late show. Nearby was the small, jet-black viola, *V.* 'Molly Sanderson'. This is a good deal blacker than the form I grow, 'Bowles Black', which – in my garden at least – reverts late in the year to a dark purple.

The house faces south-east, looking over a low valley and distant hills, which means vicious winds in winter. Many plants thrive on the walls however, including that delightful rose 'Pom Pom de Paris', threaded with the double, purple clematis, Purpurea Plena. *Parthenocissus henryana*, the Virginia Creeper, was actually in flower on the sunny side of the house, but sulking in the shade. *Genista hispanica*, bright-yellow Spanish Gorse, made a prickly mound close to the front door. I loved the owners' description of it in May, as a 'mound of butter'.

The rest of the garden consists of well planted island beds and borders, set in grass, some terraced, some with steep gradients, all merging into the encompassing woodland. Most of the beds are mixed bulbs, herbaceous perennials and

The paved garden at Farley House.

shrubs, but one is a gravel mulched bulb-bed under a huge conifer. This bed dries out completely in the wettest summer, but, as the branches of the tree are high, is in sun for part of the day. It is ideal for bulbs and corms like cyclamen, which demand a period of drought in summer for consistent flowering.

Good roses include a beautiful, single apricot, called 'Mrs Oakley Fisher', which I thought quite superb. It is one of the old hybrid tea roses of the 1930's, and can still be found at specialist nurseries (David Austin Roses, Albrighton, still stock it). A pergola supports four climbers, grown chiefly for scent. 'Sander's White', 'Auguste Gervais', 'Alister Stella Grey' and 'Adelaide d'Orleans'.

There are many interesting trees, one, *Taxodium distichum*, the Swamp Cypress, which looks a little like *Metasequoia glyptostroboides*, was chosen deliberately to inhabit a damp spot, which it loves. It is a strikingly beautiful, but *very* large conifer, which produces strange 'knees' or growths from the roots, when grown actually in water. Also unusual, was the shrub, *Bupleurum fruticosum*. It is not precisely rare, but is not often seen in gardens, probably because it is not offered frequently at garden centres. I love the shiny, evergreen leaves, and dull, greeny-yellow flowers, like a bundle of pin heads. I grow the closely related herbaceous perennial, *Bupleurum falcatum*, which looks like a small, yellow cow parsley.

I have chosen one island bed from the many to describe in detail, because it looked so fresh in the hot, dry summer. It is mostly devoted to blue and grey foliage plants, which stand up well to the heat: *Helichrysum splendens*, onopordum, the giant biennial thistle, blue rue and blue grass; but also sedums in green and purple, white shasta daisies and a most unusual, white form of the common, but beautiful weed, the Rose Bay Willow Herb, often seen on wasteground. The bed was shaded by a well-grown *Prunus serrula*, with the polished, chestnut bark, conveniently placed where one could touch as well as look.

Gatacre Park ✿ Bridgnorth

A large Victorian house set in rolling parkland, with mature rhododendrons in a woodland setting. Open under the N.G.S., see Yellow Book.

My overwhelming impressions of Gatacre are of far-flung views and the aroma of lilacs and azaleas scenting the air; though it is fair to say that every sense can be satisfied in this beautiful garden, bird song, the huge walled kitchen garden, and the soft brush of new leaves against your face in the rhododendron wood, filling in the rest of the sensual picture.

The large house stands on rising ground, with each of its four sides presenting a very different gardening experience. To begin logically at the front, the undulating lawn contains a number of island beds, each planted with a variety of shrubs and herbaceous perennials. One contains an enormous yucca, filling it entirely. Several species of this exotic evergreen are hardy in the British Isles when planted in a hot, dry, well-drained position in full sun. The specimen at Gatacre must have withstood the severe winter of 1982, and looked about to flower.

The whole of this area is protected by a mature yew hedge and light woodland. Superb specimen trees include *Acer pseudoplatanus* 'Brilliantis-simum', at its most vibrant, shrimp-pink best when we visited in mid-May, and one of the best Tulip Trees, *Liriodendron tulipifera*, in Shropshire.

Eccentric topiary at Gatacre Park.

Hidden away on the left of the lawn is a small sunken Italianate garden, with steps down to an oblong pond and six tall clipped yews. The high banks surrounding are a mixture of the difficult – *Acers palmatum* 'Dissectum', in purple and green, revelling in the cool sheltered shade, and the common – alyssum and aubrieta, blatantly yellow and mauve. A feature of this garden are the superb ornaments: a pair of leaded urns in the sunken garden, and a wonderful, marble, Grecian bowl on a tall plinth, with entwined handles and classical heads at the end of the woodland walk, mysteriously white in the green shade.

The woodland garden, with its profusion of azaleas and rhododendrons, lies to the side and front of the house. It is gardening on the largest scale and provides a perfect home for the many mature specimens including the Loderi group of rhododendrons, which are quite the finest hybrids but grow to a tremendous size. The right conditions of damp, acid soil and cool shade are imperative for these temperamental beauties, especially *R. arboreum*, the large leaved tree rhododendron.

Gatacre is renowned for its rhododendrons.

The rear of the house encompasses a sloping lawn, a ha-ha, and the view. The owners have wisely included nothing else, except to frame it with native trees and a pair of urns. It goes on and on (oh for a telescope) though one could waste a lifetime looking at it. Even the far-away tower blocks of Wolverhampton were just visible in the distant blue haze on the far right.

The right hand side of the house when facing the front holds a complete surprise. First you see a pretty iron gate, then a conventional grassed terrace with a pair of classic urns, well-filled flower beds, a superb blue cedar and steps down again to a distant prospect of serene fields, rich farmland dotted with oaks and contented cows. Here convention abruptly ends. Facing you and running the whole length of the lower terrace are a line of clipped yews: not sophisticated, classic shapes in keeping with the house, but eccentric screws, cottage garden teapots, wild teddy bears and erratic toadstools. Beautifully maintained, they dominate this side of the garden, adding that essentially British touch of humour and eccentricity to a truly delightful garden.

Glazeley Old Rectory ❀ Bridgnorth

A former rectory in rolling Shropshire countryside, sited close to the church. Open under the N.G.S., see Yellow Book.

The house at Glazeley sits comfortably on the side of a smooth hill, only a stone's throw from the eighteenth century church. The wicket gate leading from the garden to the grounds of the church immediately indicates that the house was in fact the old rectory.

It is surrounded by a typical country house garden, large and rambling, with many smaller more intricate areas, all interconnected by winding paths and gravelled drives. There is little or no formality. The entire atmosphere is of a cottage garden, in spite of the size of the house.

Its upkeep must give the present owners – who only came to the house in 1983 – nightmares. Gone are the days when the rector employed two men and a boy. Now the owners work alone with only a man to cut the grass. To simplify, or rationalise the garden, however, would be to lose half its charm. The joy comes in discovering the bog garden, with all its complicated paths and irregular beds, and the many small gardens complete with hedges which all need clipping at precisely the same time.

The church through the trees, Glazeley Old Rectory.

Close to the house is a paved area, the earth between the slabs dressed with fine chippings. Not dignified enough to be called a scree, it is nevertheless an excellent way of growing alpines or other plants which require good drainage on heavy clay soils. It works to perfection at Glazeley. I saw many evergreys, helichrysum, rue, thymes, dianthus, leontopodium, saxifraga as well as sempervivum, all flourishing in the open, well-drained gravel. Difficult alpines also appreciate the moist, cool root-run offered by the big slabs.

Spring in the orchard at Glazeley.

Many gardeners who do not have room for a lawn, or the time and the inclination to cut one regularly, might seriously consider ten tons of gravel and some paving slabs as a possible alternative. The other great advantage of a gravel mulch is weed suppression, though it goes without saying that all perennial weeds must be carefully removed first.

One cannot write about Glazeley without mentioning the primroses. The previous incumbent specialised in those frustrating beauties – the doubles, and the present owners too have continued the tradition. Glazeley has the heavy, fertile soil, the light shade and the damp which they insist on, so that the plants which slowly fade away in my garden, make superb rounded clumps covered in innumerable blooms. Double primroses were once very difficult to find, but micropropagation has totally altered the situation, and they are now readily obtainable. All plants which enjoy heavy, damp soil do well at Glazeley – rodgersia, *Iris sibirica*, caltha, hosta, trollius as well as single primroses.

In the main garden an iron pergola with wide beds on each side has been planted for high summer with the climbing rose 'Leontine Gervais'. The latter is a strong growing wichuraiana, with glossy foliage and pink flowers tinged with copper and orange. Hemerocallis, the Day Lilies, and *Helenium autumnale*, in yellow, orange and bronze shades, provide colour at ground level.

I think it must be the numerous mature apple trees which give the garden its wonderful old world air. An old apple or pear with twisted, corrugated trunk is hard to beat for character. I especially admired the tiny orchard at Glazeley – perfection, with daisies in the grass, each gnarled tree encircled by a wreath of daffodils.

The garden was on the verge of being neglected; how fortunate it is to have fallen into such loving hands.

Grindley Brook ❀ Whitchurch

A medium sized garden, containing a colourful mixture of annuals and perennials. Not open to the public.

A type of garden arose between the two world wars which one thinks of as typically suburban. At its best in high summer, it is composed of annuals, late flowering perennials like gypsophila and chrysanthemum and floriferous shrubs such as fuchsia. Geraniums and tender bulbs, begonias for example, also play a large part. This garden is now out of fashion, but it is hard to imagine a better way of treating a small area surrounding a between-the-wars house. It is ideally suited to its period, and quite as valid as a knot garden round an Elizabethan timber framed house, or carpet bedding and rhododendrons in a Victorian Gothic cottage garden.

Grindley Brook, the stream garden.

Grindley Brook falls exactly into this category, and would be hard to better for a fine show of colour in a hot, dry August. The garden is only of moderate size (about a third of an acre) and lies entirely to the front of the house. It is given interest, however, by a slope downwards to a small brook, the ground rising again on the opposite side. This is not the Grindley Brook of the garden's name, but a smaller tributary. It has been completely stone lined, and is a problem as well as an asset, because it floods badly at times.

A well built, wooden bridge crosses the river, and is in fact the only means of reaching the other side. If a bridge is not to look ridiculous it must have a purpose, this one does, and therefore fits in well with the general scheme. The owner of Grindley Brook has only just acquired the land on the further side of the river, and has spent a happy winter building the new bridge and planting up the new garden.

The garden once consisted entirely of annuals, but having a greater area to fill, and finding them prohibitively expensive, the owner has now begun to incorporate perennials into his scheme. I noted great mounds of the white daisy, *Chrysanthemum frutescens*, astilbe enjoying the damp conditions, spirea and crocosmia. Annuals included lobelia, alyssum and yellow pansies. Carnations in all shades of pink and red filled the spaces between. Superbly grown double and single hollyhocks gave height.

The garden's pièce de résistance is a wooden pergola hung from end to end with hanging baskets. The owner produces no less than two hundred every year, most of which are sold to help defray garden expenses. Only fushsias are kept from year to year, all annuals being bought in.

The soil is excellent and grows everything well. The owner states that he has dug down over two feet and still found good soil. I have certainly never seen better mimulus in a range of striking, exotic colours, spotted and plain, though they obviously love the damp

Salpiglossis, Grindley Brook.

conditions at the side of the brook. Salpiglossis are also great favourites and provide a variety of rich colours. One, in shot red and mauve, was especially eye catching. *Chrysanthemum matricaria* provided white pom-poms on compact plants to tone down the bright colours.

The only tree is a *Laburnum* × *watereri* 'Vossii', but I did not miss them, the pergola and hanging baskets helping to add interest above eye level. The owner once tried a magnolia (he didn't mention the variety) but, as it sulked for thirteen years, not growing an inch, he eventually lost patience and threw it out.

The base planting of perennials doesn't change of course, and as all the annuals disappear in the winter, the owner admits it is very much a one season garden, with little of interest in mid-winter. A new hobby fills the dark days – bonsai, which can be indulged in a cosy greenhouse!

There are many problems to face in such a thickly planted, small garden with not an inch of space uncovered. These range from the 1989 drought, water voles in the river bank, who do not stay there, but raid the carnations, and a busy main road on the other side of the garden hedge.

The beautifully maintained lawn suffered a mole invasion a year or two ago, but fortunately they were eradicated before they did too much damage. There are sweet peas on the pergola, *Lavatera* 'Pink Cloud' and 'Mont Blanc' overflowing the paths; a positive plethora of flowers everywhere. My favourite – several tubs of datura, Angels Trumpets in full bloom, their huge, exotic trumpets filling the air with scent.

The Grove ✹ Kinton

A large country garden, with magnificent views and many interesting plants. Open under the N.G.S., see Yellow Book.

There is a particular type of garden which seems very common in Shropshire: on the large side, never less than about an acre, cottage style, with profuse planting in simple, basic shapes; and with vegetables incorporated into the general scheme; usually with beautiful views, and planned around a gracious eighteenth or nineteenth century country house. Not too much emphasis on tidyness, or immaculate lawns, unusual and old-fashioned flowers growing as they please are vital elements. Perhaps most important of all, they are owned and loved by a dedicated and knowledgeable plantsman or woman. The Grove fits this pattern exactly.

The owners moved into the property in 1971 from just across the road. They admit that many neighbours wondered why they bothered, but they had coveted the beautiful, red-brick house and south-facing garden with wonderful views over the Breidden Hills for many years, and jumped at the chance to acquire it at last. Many views are called superb, but the one from The Grove really does deserve the epithet. I would even go so far as to describe it as spectacular, the rounded humps of the Breiddens rising dramatically from the flat plain.

The soil is a sandy loam, fertile, but inclined to dry out quickly in a hot summer. The beautiful eighteenth century house adds greatly to the garden picture. It is long and narrow, only seventeen feet wide, which was apparently a perfect span for an oak beam. As all of the garden is visible from every room upstairs, some emphasis has been laid on planning the garden to be viewed from above, though it strikes me as a very natural garden, that has grown, rather than been designed. An interesting historical note – the only part of the garden contempory with the house is a wide box hedge, laced with the red climbing nasturtium, or Flame Flower. This hedge was apparently planted so that the ladies of the house could visit the outside privy without being viewed by the labourers working in the fields nearby! It now neatly encompasses the top part of the vegetable garden, which – in true cottage garden tradition – sits right in the centre of the garden to take advantage of maximum light and the best soil.

The garden consists mostly of a number of long borders set in grass. The grass roughens as you approach the confines of the garden, which are concealed by mature shrubs and trees. There are many unusual plants, but I was particularly impressed at the time we visited – mid June – with the extensive collection of hardy geraniums.

These cottage garden plants par excellence are now very much in fashion. They are trouble-free, self-seeding, disease resistant and many do not need staking, or at most a few twiggy sticks pushed in around them. Rabbits ignore them, and they are bright and colourful in any soil. If they do have a fault, they are over quickly in hot weather, but the latter is sufficiently rare in this country to be overlooked. Anyway, they will grow well in partial shade, which alleviates the problem. There are many unusual forms at The Grove, but some old favourites no garden should be without are 'Johnson's Blue', a large plant with lavender-blue flowers and good, divided leaves which add interest when the flowers are over; 'Wargarve Pink', this is smaller and makes a neat tuffet

A happy association of flowers, shrubs and vegetables.

covered with bright-pink blooms; *G. phaeum*, The Mourning Widow, a good one for naturalizing; it will do well in quite deep shade. I have this one in my own garden in every shade of dark mauve to crimson, also a beautiful white, which I noted at The Grove. *G. sanguineum* – the common form is bright magenta and very lovely, but don't miss the white one 'Album', or the pink. I would also recommend the later flowering, *G. wallichianum* 'Buxton's Blue', with pale centred, cup-shaped, clear-blue flowers. This one trails, and is at its best planted on the top of a raised bed or wall.

At The Grove a tall, pale-blue cranesbill has sported a wonderful cream striped form. This was quite beautiful, and, if it could be propagated, would be a tremendous addition to the range.

To return to the main planting: the owners have arranged the beds so that they are graded for colour and time of flowering. A yellow and white border for example is at its best in early spring, having a preponderance of snowdrops and yellow-leaf shrubs. They are not dogmatic, however, and do allow other colours to creep in if they fit into the general pattern. In fact, many plants self-seed, and are permitted to choose their own environment.

The border along the house wall is wide and contains a number of tender plants. So often this bed is frustratingly narrow, even non-existent if the garden is paved and cemented to the edge. I can only suggest that you dig it up as fast as you can. A warm wall is of incalculable value, and, especially if it faces south or west, it will enable you to try all manner of exotic plants.

The white Georgian front door at The Grove is never opened. Looking at the wealth of plants growing in the paving in front of it, I can understand why. A wonderful mixture of creeping alpines vie for the limited space: *Lysimachia nummularia* 'Aurea', the yellow form of

Cotinus coggygria backing
Thalictrum speciosissinium.

Creeping Jenny, with cup-shaped yellow flowers and bright-gold leaves; The bronze four-leaf clover, *Trifolium repens* 'Purpurascens' and *Alchemilla alpina*, with silver-backed leaves. I must warn that the first two run, and the latter seeds about, but I would not be without them. Further on are lots of grey and variegated plants: common Lamb's Ear and Curry Plant, and the rare *Senecio* 'Monroi', with curled pastry case edges to its leaves, but otherwise exactly like the type plant *S. greyii*; also an amazing variegated blackberry, which I have never encountered before. This threads through a dark, evergreen ceanothus – very effective.

Other memorable combinations in other parts of the garden are *Thalictrum speciosissmum*, which is pale yellow with glaucous foliage, set against *Cotinus coggygria*, with simple, dark, plum-coloured leaves; also the single, intensely red rose, 'Altissimo', on the wall of the house. The latter could have been a disaster with the orange-red brick, were it not surrounded by *Cotoneaster horizontalis*, which provides the perfect, dark green counterpoint.

There is a small, shady area with hostas and hellebores, but this is a sunny garden, and the owners wisely go along with the conditions. The shrub roses are a joy, and do amazingly well on the light soil. There is a large collection, some rarely seen except in older gardens, or where discerning owners have sought them out. Although it is hard to grow well, and certainly not very beautiful, it was interesting to note 'Viridiflora', the Green Rose, more of a curiosity than an asset; also 'Chapeau de Napolean', an incredible crested moss, with enlarged calyx covered in green fuzz. Another perennial completely new to me was *Rhazya orientalis*. It forms a slowly increasing clump of starry, pale blue flowers on slender stems only about a foot high, and looks particularly well with the cranesbills.

In the shade of a large tree was *Digitalis parviflora*, a small foxglove with tiny, brownish-cream flowers. It seemed to me to be typical of most of the flowers in this garden, not colourful or showy, but guaranteed to get the visitors on their knees enquiring where it can be purchased.

Finally, I must mention an acre and a half, quite separate from the main garden, which the owners bought and planted as a conservation area, to counter the modern farming methods which sadly, even in Shropshire, are becoming increasingly apparent. This contains many native trees, including such rarities as quince and medlar.

Hatton Grange ✻ Shifnal

Thirty acres of widely differing garden, comprising a formal part close to the house and a large area of woodland surrounding four ponds. Open under the N.G.S., see Yellow Book.

Hatton Grange is a garden of contrasts: tailored symmentry near to the architecturally distinguished eighteenth century house; wild, mysterious, green woods, a blaze of colour at rhododendron time, well away from the main buildings and their civilizing influence.

Hatton Grange was bequeathed to the monks of Buildwas Abbey in the thirteenth century by Robert Traynell. They farmed the land and fished the four pools deep in the woods – hence the addition of 'Grange' to the name. On the dissolution of the monasteries by Henry VIII, the Grange passed through many hands until bought by the Slaneys in the seventeenth century. A descendant still lives in the house.

The monks' fishing pools form an interlinking chain, each within its own sandstone valley. Everything around them conspires to promote the sensation of great age: the spongey floor of the ancient woods, the great, grey stems of the huge beeches, the dark pools – only water in the middle of a wood can be so black – but especially the folded edges of red sandstone, making a walk there a magical experience. The claustrophobic walls of greenery press in on every side. You can touch the gritty folds of stone, some showing evidence of man's quarrying activities, other parts sculpted by nature into caves or curtain-like drapes. Only the splash of a heron stealing fish breaks the heavy silence, as he and his forebears no doubt have since the monks' time. It doesn't take a great deal of imagination to visualise the cowled figures treading the old paths as they went about their daily business.

Most of the woods consist of native trees, but there are a few exotics: more especially several mature *Acer griseum*, with torn-paper, tawny bark and wonderful autumn colour; also some magnificent *Magnolia campbellii*, the huge, goblet-shaped, pink flowers, an unforgettable sight covering a large tree. These somewhat tender giants are protected by other trees and the sides of the valley in which they grow, but it is very unusual to find them growing to such luxuriant perfection so far inland.

Passing the last pond in the chain, with its native yellow water-lilies, *Nuphar lutea*, darting dragonflies and trails of honeysuckle, the path takes an upward plunge, terminating at the top of a small hill, where one bursts out of the wood and sees a magnificent view of the house in the distance. This spot has been recently marked (in 1969) by a charming, round, pillared temple, designed by Clough Williams-Ellis, the creator of the Italianate village of Portmeirion on the North Wales coast.

Hatton Grange displaying its Georgian symmetry.

To return to the garden: the front of the house faces south-west with views to the woods (the north-west side was once the front, but was abandoned by a previous owner who objected to the internal combustion engine and effectively shut out cars with a curved wall and pretty wrought-iron gate). The new front comprises terracing with steps down to a small enclosed garden of perfect symmetry, echoing the classic Georgian facade of the house. An oblong pond is surrounded by sandstone paving, with tubs of white daisies at each corner. The plan is further emphasised by four Silver Leaf Pear – *Pyrus salicifolia* 'Pendula', underplanted with hardy geranium.

The rose garden lies to the south-east, and is enclosed by clipped yew hedges. It has recently been renovated and now contains many old-fashioned shrub roses. One enters under arches draped with the climbers 'Madame Alfred Carrière', a strong growing old rose, with sweetly scented flesh-pink blooms, and climbing 'Sombreuil', a flat, quartered old rose in creamy-white with a strong scent.

The orange-red brick walls of the house are not neglected. I noted a beautiful, unnamed, white climbing rose, something like a noisette, with small, very double flowers; also that great, white climber, *R. filipes* 'Kiftsgate' romping over an adjacent build-ing. This does need a whole building or large tree to itself to display its full glory.

I must mention a beautifully grown *Clematis orientalis* 'Bill Mackenzie' against the gar-dener's annex. This has quite the largest flowers of any form; many yellow, thick-petalled blooms with black centres, set against the lovely, ferny foliage, demonstrating very well how im-portant it is to make the effort to get hold of the best form of a plant.

Stone 'curtains' near the lakes at Hatton Grange.

There is a further area of semi-wild garden towards the back of the house dotted with magnificent specimen trees and large swathes of uncut grass, a home to naturalized bulbs earlier in the year and full of wild flowers later, including wild orchids. The grass here is never cut until July.

I was charmed by the square dovecote, which provides a vertical element at the end of a long wall. This outside wall of the kitchen garden, now utilized for a small plantation of Christmas trees, provides ideal protection for many tender plants. These include a *Piptanthus laburnifolius*, a member of the pea family, with broom-like, yellow flowers. The common, furry Lambs Ear, *Stachys olympica* makes a ribbon of grey ground cover at its feet.

Martin Elson the gardener is a young and enthusiastic member of a team devoted to preserving the beauty and unique atmosphere of this beautiful garden.

Haughmond ❀ Felton Butler

A one acre garden with interesting wild life area. Open under the N.G.S., see Yellow Book.

The garden at Haughmond is living evidence to set against the canard that farmers do not make good gardeners. It is a new garden, set in the middle of what was once an open field, packed to bursting with all kinds of perennials, shrubs and trees. The owner admits that she packs plants in far too tightly, as she hates the sight of bare earth. Fortunately, when things get out of hand, she can commandeer a further expanse of field.

The owner likes to live dangerously. I noted several plants which I have only dared attempt in a cold greenhouse. These include pittosporum from Australia, evergreen shrubs or small trees with delightful, crinkly foliage, some variegated – ideal for flower arrangements. They do have scented flowers, though these are small. A callistemon or Bottle Brush was also in full bloom. This is another evergreen, sun-lover, from Australia, whose name exactly describes the round flower spikes, which are composed entirely of stamens. *C. saligrus* is one of the hardiest forms – if you are prepared to take a chance: it has pale yellow flowers and narrow, willow-like leaves. I prefer the red forms, especially *C. citrinus* 'Splendens', which is bright scarlet. You could compromise by growing it in a pot and moving it indoors during the winter.

A Passion Flower, *Passiflora caerulea*, is ideally placed on the south-facing front of the house. This is rather more hardy than the two previously mentioned shrubs, but can still be lost in a bad winter. It is somewhat rampant in growth, with dark-green, palmate leaves. A good tip – buy a named variety, not one raised from seed, otherwise you may be disappointed with its flowering performance. If it is cut down in a bad winter, don't dig it up too soon. It often shoots again, better than ever for its enforced pruning.

I noted some delightful trees set in the wide lawn. One, the Silver Leaf Pear, was host for that good, pink *Clematis* 'Hagley Hybrid'. The colour combination was lovely. A gleditsia looked wonderful against the dark-green of conifers, its beautiful, yellow

The wild garden at Haughmond.

foliage glowing in the hot sun. This was the very striking form known as 'Sunburst', though there are others equally good. The owner has a definite penchant for red foliage, which forms a background for many of the herbaceous perennials, and comes in the form of *Cotinus coggygria* 'Royal Purple', as well as the red *Berberis* 'Rosy Glow', and *B.* × *ottowensis* 'Purpurea'. The annual, Red Orach, beloved of cottage gardeners and flower arrangers, also seeds itself around and provides another splash of dark red.

Plants are so tight that very little staking needs to be done, each group holding up another. One very attractive combination was the tall, grey *Artemisia ludoviciana*, threaded through vinca and a lovely, pink cistus. This artemisia is both a runner *and* a flopper, so is always difficult to place.

Pink and grey seems another favourite colour combination of the owner, as I also saw a *Eucalyptus gunnii* – one of the most hardy of the Gum Trees – fronted by the new *Buddleia* 'Delight'. The latter is a gorgeous sugar-pink, really different, and should be in every buddleia lover's garden.

Quite separate from the garden, around the back of the house, is a natural area given over entirely to providing a home for wild life.

The pond is almost hidden in the bullrushes and long grass, but teems with frogs, toads and dragonflies. Wild flowers abound in the long grass. The only cultivated area, apart from the mown grass walks, is a half-moon shaped bed of herbs. This included many annuals, which I personally never get around to sowing in time, but are pretty plants, purslane, coriander and summer savory, especially, have the most delicate foliage. Also looking good was a great block of feverfew, hyssop, nepeta and fennel.

An interesting hedge, which hides a plastic greenhouse, is grown entirely from rugosa hips. This means that the flowers are sometimes not perfect and do not match, which is why for perfect symmetry, a hedge should always be raised from cuttings, if possible, from the same plant. In a wild area, however, the rose hedge looks just right, and I think the differences add to its charm.

There are small, silver willows to give height, but this is a true conservation plot, and does not pretend to be anything else. At the far side of the garden are a number of pens containing badgers which have been injured. The owners accepted one many years ago, when it was presented with a broken leg to a local vet. They nursed it back to health, then let it go. Inevitably, they are now the recipients of all the injured badgers in this part of Shropshire. The first badger sparked their interest in conservation, however, and it is now a full scale hobby, with well thought out lectures and slides.

Another pen holds a fox, which was stolen from the wild, tamed and then discarded. The owner of Haughmond took it on as it was too used to humans to release. Now, as she gardens in the cool of the evening, it follows her around. I can't think of a better companion in her wildlife haven.

Haye House ✿ Eardington

A one acre flower arranger's garden, replanned and replanted over the past ten years. Open under the N.G.S., see Yellow Book.

Haye House is a fascinating building, set high on an escarpment overlooking the River Severn. It has an interesting history, being part red sandstone – built 1525, and part Georgian brick – built 1725. The two halves blend perfectly, helped by an abundance of climbers growing over both back and front of the house.

The owner is a renowned international flower arranger, who had just returned from a world trip encompassing destinations as diverse as Germany and Hong Kong. This passion for flower arranging shows in the garden, with special emphasis on good foliage and superbly planted urns.

The garden is one of the last to open for the National Garden Scheme, in late July, and I wondered whether anything would still be out when we visited on a blistering hot day in one of the driest summers on record. I need not have worried, as the garden

An object lesson in how to plant up urns from Haye House.

looked delightful, being one of the very few which included annuals in the general planting scheme.

The great divide among gardeners today is whether or not to grow annuals. I am defining annuals here as a plant which will not overwinter outside in our climate. The arguments rage on either side. Those who do not like annuals are plant snobs. Those who do are accused of poor taste, and producing a riot of colour at the expense of subtlety. At the moment the poor old annual is going through a bad time. It is supposedly unsophisticated, unfashionable, cheap and cheerful, while all trendy gardeners are striving for the country garden, muted, toned-down effect. I hate annuals in stiff, colour-clashing rows (as I would any plant); but blended in with perennials, in well thought out blocks of colour, they can prolong the growing season into a fallow August, especially in a hot, dry summer like the one experienced in 1989. In large pots, tubs and urns they are quite unbeatable, except that you have to start anew every year, and *have* to feed and water regularly, giving them a head start in dry weather.

The urns at Haye House are very beautiful and added greatly to the garden picture. The basic planting is the classic one of geraniums with grey-green *Helichrysum petiolatum* as a foil. Diversity comes from the shades of red among the geraniums, which ranged from that vibrantly intense vermilion, through true red to a white edged with pink. Outside the garden a long horse trough used grey *Senecio cineraria*, dwarf fuchsia and more geraniums. Some natural stone troughs featured a complete contrast: dwarf conifers in many different shades of green, various leaf textures and of either rounded, prostrate or conical habit.

A large island bed in the flat front lawn also featured annuals, here mixed in blocks of colour, with background shrubs and perennials. These included pansies, grey artemisia, that wonderful, variegated plant *Scrophularia aquatica* 'Variegata', pink delphiniums and *Potentilla* 'Pretty Polly', also pink. Height came from *Acer* 'Flamingo', a glorious concoction of white, pink and cream, and the dark-plum, *Cotinus coggygria* 'Royal Purple', always a superb background plant.

The owner seems to have a penchant for pansies, as blocks of one colour, planted in small circular beds, surround specimen trees on the front lawn.

The garden slopes upwards from the side of the house and features a number of low, clipped hedges, as well as terracing walls. The owner informed me that many dead rhododendrons and briars had to be cleared from this area when she acquired the house eleven years ago. Now it is well laid out with specimen trees and shrubs, most chosen for good foliage as well as flower. The soil is excellent, a clayey loam, so that everything grows vigorously, and, even on a steep slope in dry weather, manages to retain moisture.

There is a quite beautiful urn at the side of the house, just where the slope begins, planted not only with geranium and helichrysum, but also an exotic, spiky yucca. The base of the yucca is hidden in foliage, so that it appears to rise out of the planting and float above.

There is an interesting, oblong pond, with a dolphin fountain at each end, surrounded on three sides by a wall and a number of mysterious, shady, gravel paths behind it. These lead to the top of the slope and the vegetable garden.

Once among the vegetables, the owners' occupation is again apparent, as it has far more rows of flowers for cutting than things to eat. Sweet peas dominate, but I noted a great block of *Amaranthus caudatus*, with long tassels of blood-red flowers. I had never really considered annuals for cutting before, except for the sweet peas, but am now alert to the possibilities after seeing them at Haye House.

A final point: I thought I was the only person who dragged home driftwood, old tree trunks and pieces of stone discovered on various outings around the country, but the owner of Haye House also indulges in this hobby (they are of course ideal in flower arrangements). I would have dearly loved some of the sculptured driftwood in this garden, which decorated the borders in happy relationship with the flowers.

Hazler Croft ❀ Church Stretton

A perfect suburban garden covering a quarter of an acre in a small town setting. No longer open to the public.

My first thought after walking round the garden at Hazler Croft was that I would not change a single object in it, not a plant, ornament or tree. It is quite perfect: a visual object lesson in how to plan and plant a small area surrounding a modern house.

The owner has lived there for six years, and, on moving in, was faced with the usual square plot, encircled by the obligatory straight, narrow border and uninspired planting. She sought first to disguise the acute angles and hard rims that defined and regularized the plot by creating a curved edge to the border against a background of evergreen conifers. These also served to blot out the neighbouring houses and mute the traffic noise from the nearby A49. It is hard to believe one is so close to the centre of Church Stretton. Blue hills stretch into the distance in one direction. Superb mature limes across the road block out the houses in another.

There are many good shrubs and trees in the garden; some carefully chosen for slow, compact growth, such as *Acer pseudoplatanus* 'Brilliantissimum', *Crataegus orientalis sanguinea*, *Stranvaesia davidiana* 'Palette', as well as the more common japonicas, kolkwitzia and deutzias; others, *Pyrus salicifolia* 'Pendula', the Silver Leaf Pear and *Rosa rubrifolia* carefully pruned to fit in.

Towards the front of the borders are many dwarf rhododendron and azalea. A large *Cotoneaster horizontalis* runs the full length of one wall of the bungalow. This is never pruned, as its chief beauty lies in the herring-bone pattern of its branches and the owner has carefully chosen a site where it can grow unrestricted to its maximum size.

There is a well planted, carefully placed pond with a fountain, and a terrace with low walls close to the house. *Clematis montana* 'Grandiflora'

Hazler Court, water gardening in a small area.

47

Anthemis cupaniana in the perfect position.

Lead statue at Hazler Croft.

grows on a corner of the house, a better choice than the more common pink for difficult shades of brick. At the rear of the house where the previous occupants grew raspberries and vegetables, the owner has created a circular raised garden, the interior paved, the outside edges hung with herbaceous perennials. I have never seen *Anthemis cupaniana* better grown. Usually one is exhorted to let its mound of feathery grey leaves topped with white daisies sprawl over a path, but I shall now advise planting on the top of the raised bed. Also noted in this grouping was a subtly shaded mauve cow parsley, or Queen Anne's Lace.

Beautifully mossed stone toadstools and a curious round font or old farm feeding trough form an integral part of the design in this area. In fact, this garden could be admired for the beautifully placed and aesthetically satisfying garden ornaments alone. Ornaments can make or break the overall visual experience in a small garden, so often they are tasteless and crude. No matter how good the planting, many turn the small garden into a disaster area, spoiling a good scheme. Garden ornaments should reflect the size and general setting of the house. If you would like a piece of garden sculpture, far better to commission a local artist, who will view the site and create something in keeping, than spend a small fortune on a mass produced, Greek style statue.

Hazler Croft is a good example of how garden ornaments should be chosen and placed, with all the limitations a small site and a modern house impose.

Hodnet Hall ✿ Hodnet

A Shropshire lakeland landscape in miniature. Open daily April to September inclusive.

I think it was a Rothschild who confidently stated that no *small* garden should be without its five or six acres of natural woodland, proving yet again that everything in this life is relative. By anyone's standards, however, Hodnet Gardens are huge: over sixty acres with a vast area of daffodil and bluebell strewn woodland. In fact, the overall impression I have of Hodnet is an unforgettable combination of large trees and much water. Not that colour is wanting. During our spring visit, acers and rhododendrons supplied all that one could desire in abundance. The hot, sugar-pink of *Azalea* 'Hinomayo', shining yellow of the well-known, common luteum (still unbeatable for fragrance) and the vibrant orange of the Exbury azaleas dazzled the eye. Reflections in the water, subtle shades of green and blue toned and blended to produce an impressionist picture.

Hodnet was planned around a chain of lakes created in 1922 out of a marshy hollow. Looking at its mature perfection today it is almost impossible to believe that it is not natural, so well does the water fit the landscape.

The gardens were planted to provide something of interest throughout the year, starting with the vast sheets of daffodils in early spring, followed by rhododendrons and azaleas, then all the high summer flowers in their turn, with an emphasis of course on the plants which thrive in a damp garden, such as candelabra primulas, ferns, the mighty gunnera, astilbes and *Iris kaempferi*. As befits a garden with so many rare and exotic trees, the show of autumn colour and berries is almost as spectacular as the spring display.

The soil at Hodnet is a stiff, fertile clay, but here and there the underlying bones of the garden in the shape of great lumps of red sandstone push themselves to the surface. No attempt has been made to remove the stone. Instead, the rocky outcrops have been incorporated into the display. Narrow steps, painstakingly chiselled out of

Hodnet is noted for its early display of azaleas and rhododendrons.

49

solid rock lead to mysterious rhododendron hung paths. Not the least of Hodnet's charms is the unexpected vignette of a stone gateway, far-away dovecote or a Victorian summerhouse half hidden in the trees contrasting with the wide spaciousness of the lakes and lawns.

For such a large garden the standard of maintenance is incredible: lawns a velvety green perfection, gravel paths weed-free and freshly raked. What joy to gaze into the crystal-clear water; even catch sight of a giant carp carefully working over the bottom for scraps of food, and, to complete the picture, a black swan and three white ducks.

Hodnet is home to some of the largest and most impressive trees in Shropshire: among them, a *Metasequoia glyptostroboides*; a huge larch-*Larix decidua*, which from its size must be one of the earliest planted; a fastigiate hornbeam, *Carpinus betulus fastigiata*, easily grown trees suitable for heavy clay; weeping beech, *Fagus sylvatica pendula*; mighty oaks; the Oriental Plane, *Platanus orientalis* and a giant walnut.

These are only the larger specimens. For the garden also holds many of the more ornamental, smaller trees suitable for private gardens on a more modest scale. There is a collection of cherries near the lake including *Prunus* 'Okame', 'Accolade', 'Hisakura', 'Ukon' (a large tree) 'Pendula Rubra' (the best weeper) and the fastigiate 'Amanogawa'.

Hodnet Hall.

The acers are superb, revelling in the moist atmosphere emitted from the great sheets of water, and sheltered by the large trees and the natural lie of the land. There are wonderful magnolias, a large flowered form of the Snowdrop Tree, *Halesia monticola*, probably 'Vestita'; a superb variety with flowers sometimes 3 cm across, white tinged with rose in some forms. There are *Liquidamber styraciflua*, *Parrotia persica* and *Cercidiphyllum japonicum* for autumn colour. But for me, the glory of the garden is the *Davidia involucrata* or Pocket-handkerchief Tree.

This is a medium size tree with not very big flowers, but each head has a pair of white bracts hanging downwards exactly like a handkerchief. It is perfectly hardy, but slow to mature; the sight of a full grown specimen in May is well worth waiting for however.

It was in the woodland area at Hodnet that I first saw trilliums growing en masse. They enjoy cool, moist positions in fertile soil, so Hodnet suits them to perfection, and they reward the owner by producing their three petalled, three leafed flowers every year in early spring. *Trillium grandiflorum*, 'Wake Robin', is perhaps the best known, but the reddish *T. chloropetalum* with a ruff of mottled, dark green leaves grows best at Hodnet. All the trilliums are natives of the United States, expensive to buy and slow of increase, but, like the Davidia, well worth the time and trouble.

I have not mentioned the kitchen garden, the great Tithe Barn, beautifully restored and worth a visit on its own or the amazing collection of pre-war big game trophies in the Tearoom and the nursery where plants from the garden can be purchased.

I have visited Hodnet many times at all seasons of the year and find it that rare achievement, a garden which always has something to enjoy.

Inga Pengar ❀ Oswestry

A small suburban garden, containing a comprehensive and well laid out collection of herbaceous perennials. Open under the N.G.S., see Yellow Book.

By mid-July, especially after a blistering hot, dry summer, most gardens would be looking distinctly tired. Not so the garden at Inga Pengar. It is a typical, small, suburban plot, made somewhat more difficult to plan, as the ground slopes downwards towards the house – always a tricky proposition when designing a garden. A further problem, is the huge, pink-flowered horse chestnut, which dominates the front of the house. Fortunately, it is some way from any buildings, and the problem has been turned into an asset by careful choice of plant material in the dry, shady border beneath its branches.

Thoughtful choice of herbaceous perennials and shrubs is in fact the hallmark of this garden. There are rarities of course, but it is the high standard of cultivation that impresses: the attention to detail that allows every plant to give of its best; staking, ultimate size, habit of growth and colour combinations being carefully considered before a plant is placed in the ground.

Meticulous cultivation of herbaceous border, Inga Pengar.

Most of the ornamental garden lies to the front of the house. This is laid out with one straight border along the drive, and a series of island beds set into a large and immaculately maintained lawn. Smaller beds nestling under the house walls are ideal for tender subjects, and utilized to the full. A watsonia caught my eye in this tender bed. It is superficially like a large crocosmia, and needs to be planted deep to survive. Otherwise it can be lifted like a gladiolus and stored for the winter and is definitely worth trying. I greatly admired the orange-red, funnel shaped flowers and rush-like leaves.

Also in this bed, but not at all tender, was a superb dicentra with mauvy-green, ferny leaves and pinky-mauve flowers. The subtlety of the colour combination was quite breathtaking.

The island beds hold delightful groups of plants. I particularly liked the leaves of *Hosta fortunei albopicta* and 'Aureo-Marginata', both flowering well, thus giving twice the garden value; also in this bed were *Astible* 'Fanal', a dark-crimson red and the tall perennial *Lobelia*, 'Dark Crusader', a dark-red again. There were several white flowers for contrast: *Chrysanthemum maximum* 'Snow Dwarf', a lovely compact form and the white *C. matricaria* 'Bridal Robe'. Other reds come from the *Penstemon* 'Garnet' – in my opinion, one of the very few truly hardy forms – and a tall, brilliant vermilion lychnis. The latter is hard to place, as the colour is so startling, but the surrounding muted reds tone it down perfectly.

The garden is sited on heavy, damp, retentive clay, and this must account for all the moisture loving plants doing so well in the exceptionally dry summer. The rear of the house slopes downwards towards a small river running in a deep, walled gully. There are more large trees here which helps to isolate the garden from its near neighbours, giving a rural feel even in a suburban street.

Half of the back garden is given over to the river, greenhouse, vegetables and soft fruit, but there is still room for yet more herbaceous perennials. As the slope is greatest at the rear, the ground has been terraced. One tall wall, which holds back the soft fruit garden, has a delightful edge of *Nepeta* 'Souvenir d'Andre Chaudron', sometimes called 'Blue Beauty'. The top of a wall, or cascading over a path, are really the only ways to grow this notorious 'flopper'. It looks perfect at Inga Pengar.

An unusual very big tree in this part of the garden is the Canadian Oak, with large, yellowish leaves. A newly planted *Liquidamber styraciflua*, with maple-like leaves is noted for its super autumn colour. I guessed it might be frustrating for the owner – who is a noted plantswoman – to have to cram all she wanted into such a small area, and she did admit that it was difficult to keep colour schemes going throughout the year. She is very selective however. Anything which does not fit has to go. She also tends to select plants with good foliage, and in the blue, soft-yellow, white, pink and mauvey-red regions. Vibrant orange and yellow are rarely sought, which does help the overall picture. She makes notes on moving plants around and lists plant she would like to acquire. If the plant stays on the list, or appears several times, she usually buys it.

Some lovely plants at the back of the house included *Achillea* 'Lilac Beauty' (the new Bressingham Hybrids are also excellent) and several more lobelia, 'Tanya' and 'Will Scarlet'. These latter two *are* tender, but have survived two winters, and one can always overwinter a few cuttings in the greenhouse. Of similar hardiness are the phygelius, shrubs in warmer climates, but cut down like herbaceous perennials in colder areas. They flower all summer, especially against a sunny wall, where the stems are laden with tiny trumpets in soft coral and red. There is also a good yellow form, 'Yellow Trumpet'.

There are many more excellent plants in this garden, too numerous to mention, but all grown to perfection.

Joydene ❀ Broseley

A beautifully maintained, medium sized garden, on a sloping site. Not open to the public.

One or other half of a husband and wife team often dominates in a garden, the female half sometimes inclining to a cottage effect and the male to annuals and vegetables. At Joydene, the garden is a real partnership of equals. The garden is large for the form of layout preferred – a mixture of perennials and annuals. The work involved growing on such a vast number of dahlias, fuchsia, French Marigolds, antirrhinum and godetia every year is mind boggling. Nothing is bought in; all are produced in the two small greenhouses, discreetly hidden behind the runner beans at the top of a slope.

The owners have lived in the bungalow (which they built themselves) for twenty-eight years. The site was unpromising: a hillside of builders' ash and old clay workings, overgrown with conifers. Nothing was retained but some apple trees from an old orchard, which makes a good green background for the garden. The front is long and narrow and has been logically developed with a central path, and two parallel lawns on each side. The borders which separate the path from the grass are a golden-bronze river of French Marigolds, interspersed with standard fuchsia in full flower. There are fifteen on each side, making a flamboyant show. My favourite is 'Thalia', of the long, orange-scarlet, tube-shaped flowers. The owner tells me it is the most difficult to train as a standard, as it insists on branching all the way up the stem. Hanging baskets on the house were planted up with the yellow Canary Creeper, *Tropaeolum peregrinum*, grown from seed, which made an effective trailer.

The rear garden is set on a steep hillside, and, at over an acre, is one of the largest private gardens devoted almost entirely to annuals I have ever seen. One or two perennials are grown, and conifers help to give shape out of season, but a completely different winter scheme is put in place every year.

All the stone used for terracing and the rock gardens came from Wenlock Edge, and therefore blends in well; though it can hardly be seen between and beneath the plants. Some creeping, perennial ground cover at the edges of the garden include vinca, sedums and Lamium galeobdolon; but they are all kept strictly under control by severe clipping several times a year.

Profuse planting round a well-placed pool at Joydene.

I greatly admired the superb plumbago, *P. capensis*, grown in a pot against a sunny wall. This beautiful, pale blue plant will climb if helped with a frame, and produces its bunches of flowers freely all summer. It must be brought in during the winter, however; so perhaps its best place is in a conservatory border.

There is a well landscaped fish pond close to the patio, with carefully graded plants, again terraced with Wenlock stone. I loved the Monkey Puzzle tree, *Araucaria araucana*. One rarely sees this Victorian favourite planted now, but it can make a good centre piece. Cold winters tend to defoliate the lower trunk and branches, but in a sheltered aspect, it is often clothed right down to the ground, when it is as beautiful as any conifer. The leaves make a fascinating spiral round the branches, as do the branches round the trunk. The underplanting was of nasturtiums in red, orange and yellow, which the owner never bothers to set as they seed themselves every year.

Dahlias were once a speciality of this garden, and several rows for cutting remain, perfectly grown with large flowers and glossy foliage, in a mixture of pom-pom, cactus and plain. My all time favourite dahlia is 'Bishop of Landaff', with single, scarlet flowers and very dark foliage. It was once unobtainable, but can now be purchased from good nurseries. It is of course, tender, like all dahlias, and must be stored in a dry, frost free shed over winter. An alternative system, if you don't want to disturb big clumps, is to mulch with a good mound of peat or bracken, and take a chance – always making sure you have replacement cuttings in the greenhouse.

There are many more interesting fuchsia at the rear of the house. These too are worth experimenting with, if you don't object to losing a few. I have often been pleasantly surprised at how many, when left out all winter, came through, making new growth from below ground like a herbaceous plant. You are in the hands of your own garden's micro-climate, and the severity of the winter of course.

There was once an old cottage at the back of the bungalow, but the owners purchased it, demolished it (utilizing the stone) and gained more garden. They have plans for a summerhouse at the top of the slope where the cottage once sat, as it has a superb view of Benthall Edge, the only one in the garden. They tell me that if they ever need any bricks, all they have to do is dig on the site of the old cottage.

There are a few shrubs in this part of the garden, which also accommodates the vegetables, cotoneaster, lavender and H.T. roses, but the main theme of the garden is annuals. The two greenhouses close by are a reminder that, as soon as Christmas is over, the whole process of growing on the plants starts all over again.

Landscape ❀ near Knockin

A large natural garden planned with conservation in mind. Not open to the public.

Landscape is a bird watcher's paradise. Half an acre of formal lawn and herbaceous border is surrounded by another three consisting of mature trees and rough grass. The latter is cut only after the wild flowers and bulbs have seeded.

The great variety of conifers, deciduous trees and large shrubs mean that many species of birds abound naturally, but they are also encouraged by the provision of breeding places. I was fascinated to see a nesting hole for a nuthatch (occupied) built into a wall, and a tier of swift nests which have to be closed all winter with polystyrene to keep the starlings out. Swifts screamed and dive-bombed overhead as we looked around the garden, proving that it is a successful ploy.

In the nearby meadow wild flowers flourish, while goldfinches helped themselves to the plentyful seeds of dandelion and thistle. Owls nest in the tall Scot's Pine bordering the long drive. Mistle thrushes strip the berries from the holly and every kind of tit except the bearded visit throughout the year. A delightful round pond provides a breeding ground for dragonfly and frogs. There were only a few butterflies at the season we visited, but with a wide assortment of sweet-scented shrubs, buddleias, syringa, lilac and choisya, as well as herbaceous perennials of simple, daisy shape and many sedums, there must be hundreds later in the year. The owners do admit to some spraying, but always with care and consideration for the wildlife.

They speak disparagingly of the soil, which is the hungry, acid sand of Knockin Heath, dry as a bone in summer and needing constant mulching to produce anything approaching fertility. From the size and the luxuriant growth of the trees and shrubs however, I feel there must be something in the soil; though two mild winters followed by two damp summers will have helped.

When the owners moved into the property over forty years ago, the 1920's house sat in the middle of a field. They laid out the entire garden themselves. Maintenance has been a problem in later years, but keeping the area near the house tidy, and allowing the surrounds partially to revert to nature seems an excellent solution to the problem of reliable help.

There is a definite line between the more cultivated garden and the wilder parts. On one side of the boundary is a long border containing many old-fashioned herbaceous perennials as well as bulbs and small shrubs, and on the other, a terraced wall of sandstone and a line of tall shrubs. I noted two delightful philadelphus; one very tall, vigorous, suckering shrub which I have often seen in old gardens – it has the most wonderful fragrance; the other, a small bush with tiny, delicate blooms, also with a strong perfume. Choicer shrubs close to the house include a large chimonanthus, or Winter Sweet, very well placed under a window, where its wonderful scent in the dark days of winter can be fully appreciated. The owners admit it would be a great deal larger if it was not regularly plundered for vases in the house. Other quality shrubs include halesia, *Cornus kousa* and exochorda, all of which seem to have done exceptionally well all over

Perfect blending of the wild and cultivated.

55

the county in 1989.

An interesting ivy growing on the garden wall, *Hedera helix* 'Sagittifolia', with long points like an arrow, came from a cutting taken at Highgate Cemetery. One gets the impression that most of the garden grew in this way, rather than wholesale orders from large nurseries.

I noted a clever way of growing herbs at the top of the herbaceous border close to the house (where they are instantly available for the pot). A brick framework of small squares had been constructed many years ago, and was now beautifully weathered. In each compartment grew real French tarragon, sages, rue, feverfew – the yellow kind which is much prettier – chives and the variegated pineapple mint. The latter is one of the best variegated plants in any garden, and well worth a place at the front of the herbaceous border.

All the good, old-fashioned perennials grow in the wide mixed border: poppies, dicentra, foxgloves in white, and a subtle raspberry shade, phlox, *Euphorbia griffithii* 'Fireglow', astrantia, delphinium, hosta and many more. This herbaceous bed is also heavily mulched regularly, but the owners state that it disappears almost as soon as it is put on.

At the bottom of the garden a low wall, topped with a lavender hedge and bisected by steps, leads to a rough area of grass dotted with shrub roses. A circle of clear earth is kept around their roots, and this too is mulched to conserve moisture. I noted 'Canary Bird' – a clear, single yellow rose with lovely foliage, 'Clair Matin', 'Aloha', *Rosa complicata*, 'Conrad Ferdinand Meyer' and a beautiful specimen of 'Cerise Bouquet'. The latter also has small, neat leaves and open sprays of cerise-pink flowers on long, arching stems.

Iris have a border to themselves close to the lavender hedge. Always a good idea as they are a here today, gone tomorrow plant, difficult to place in the main planting scheme. The biggest *Cornus mas* I have ever seen grows nearby. It must be a wonderful sight in flower.

Three complete surprises, which prove the garden must be warmer and more fertile than the owners suspect are Indigofera, with small, purple pea flowers throughout the summer (it can be cut in a severe winter but usually recovers), *Ribes alpinum* 'Aureum', the yellow flowering currant, and a *Liquidamber styraciflua* for autumn colour.

Lea House ✿ Albrighton

A collection of trees and rhododendron, surrounding a modern house and a large pond. No longer open to the public.

What an asset a natural source of water is in a garden, be it pond, marsh, river or lake. Lea House is fortunate in having a good sized, well sited, marl pit in the large two acre garden, surrounding the square 1925 house. The soil is sand, overlying a fertile clay, and the latter was once much prized for spreading on farm land. To this end, large quantities were dug out in the past, creating semi-natural ponds, some of considerable size and many feet deep. The marl pit at Lea House must have a hidden source of water as, although it suffers in an exceptional year, it never dries up completely.

We saw the garden late in the season, when the huge oak overhanging the pond reflected darkly in the deep green water, the occasional plop of a falling acorn startlingly loud on a still autumnal day. Although the water *had* receded, exposing a beach round a small island (where the many ducks on the pond roost overnight to escape the depredations of foxes) the plantings round the edge still looked in reasonable condition. They appreciate the legacy of moisture held in the clay soil, as well as the welcome shade cast by the giant oak. I noted astilbes, over now, but with delicate, ferny foliage, and an excellent polygonum, something like a cross between milletti with dark red pokers and superbum with tall, pale pink spikes. All the foliage of this type of polygonum looks like that of a dock, but they are invaluable plants for any damp, semi-wild area. I would also recommend *P. affine*, for top class ground cover – dozens of small pokers, shading from pink, through red, to rust, as they mature, rising out of a weed resistant mat of leaves.

Rudbeckia *'Goldsturm'*,
Lea House.

I think one naturally gravitates towards the water in any garden, but there are many more delights at Lea House. Well placed summer-houses dot the garden, making sitting out a pleasure in most weather conditions. One, close to the pond, is a classic form in rustic logs, dating it is believed from about 1916. It was once thatched and boasted stained glass windows, but although these are long gone it still retains its old world charm.

I was especially impressed with the wide range or rare and interesting trees. Some are as yet immature, but much thought and planning has gone into their choice, planting and display. I had never come across *Betula lenta* before, but have now added it to my, 'Plants to be acquired' list. Unlike most birch, it has a dark, reddish-purple bark, but its chief glory is the brilliant yellow of its autumn display. Also chosen for autumn colour is *Nyssa sylvatica*; as it resents disturbance, only a small specimen as yet. It comes from North America, and the owner states that its autumn tinge of yellow, orange and scarlet is quite breathtaking. Close by was one of the best specimens of *Parrotia persica* I have ever seen. It is more like a large shrub than a tree, forming a mound of down turning branches (I believe there is a form called 'Pendula', but they all seem to exhibit this habit of growth to some extent). One would not normally give it a second glance throughout most of the year, but all changes when it becomes a blaze of reddish-orange late in the season. It is not easy to establish, nor cheap to buy, but well worth a place of honour in any garden, large or small.

Acer negundo 'Flamingo' is perhaps the best known

Lea House, *'mini arboretum'*.

of the Box Elders, but the owners of Lea House recommend *A. n.* 'Variegatum' instead. They find that 'Flamingo', although dramatic in pink, cream and green when small, loses its colour as it matures, while 'Variegatum' in plain green and white improves. Both these trees tend to revert incidentally, so prune carefully.

The grass, in what I can only describe as the mini-arboretum, is cut throughout the year with a variety of mowers. The owners leave the grass where it lies, unless they wish to make a particular effort to display the garden at its best, or it has become too long. When the grass is removed, it is used for mulching; though all newly planted trees and shrubs are fitted with a collar of black plastic to retain moisture and suppress weed growth.

Two more trees must be described before we leave this area, a *Gleditsia triacanthos* or Honey Locust, with the most vicious spines in large groups all the way up the trunk (it does have elegant, frond-like leaves as a compensation) also *Hoheria glabrata*, from New Zealand, which produces a stunning display of white flowers in mid-summer. This plant is a little tender, something akin to the hebes, which also come from New Zealand, but well worth a warm wall or a sheltered site in the open garden.

It is so easy to become obsessed with the beautiful trees to the exclusion of everything else, but I must mention a delightful planting of dwarf rhododendron close to the pond, protected from ducks' feet by a low, green fence. How sensible to group the smaller rhododendrons, as some are really tiny, and would be swamped by their larger relations. This bed has an unusual edging of dwarf, clump-forming thymes, such as 'Silver Posy'.

Another interesting planting close to the gates, again overshadowed by a magnificent Western Hemlock, a Tulip Tree and a Turkey Oak – the latter already a glorius dull crimson – include a variety of mahonias under-planted with ivy. Ivy makes excellent ground cover, as well as climbing tree, wall or house. The owners of Lea House have chosen 'Glacier' – a subtle, grey-green and white, 'Paddy's Pride' – large, glossy-green leaves, with yellow veining, 'Heise Denmark' – greeny-cream, with a rounded leaf and 'Chester' – which I don't know, but looks similar to 'Glacier'. My personal favourite 'Goldheart', with bright-gold and green colouring, was excluded, as a beautiful specimen covers an entire north wall close to the house.

I have concentrated on the trees in the garden, but there is also a comprehensive collection of rhododendrons for early colour, many interesting herbaceous perennials and a large group of alpines, including a well-grown specimen of that most difficult to please daphne, *D. cneorum* 'Variegata'. Altogether a most delightful garden at any season of the year.

Limeburners ✻ Ironbridge

A large ten acre garden, designed to make the most of a challenging, sloping site on the side of the Ironbridge Gorge. Open under the N.G.S., see Yellow Book.

Visiting Limeburners today, it is almost impossible to believe that its origins were a refuse tip. The owners, who began the work of reclamation in 1970, had not only the usual rubbish to contend with, but compacted foundry sand and other industrial waste. One can only admire their pluck, although it was a four person job, with two sons able and willing to lend a hand, or in some cases, a pickaxe!

As the whole family is keenly interested in conservation with a special emphasis on entomolgy, the main aim was to create a garden attractive to butterflies and moths as well as other insects. No attempt therefore has been made to have a consistently tidy garden. The cultivated parts near the house merge seamlessly with the rougher areas of woodland, gorse and flower dotted meadow.

A great deal of the soil around Ironbridge is well-drained, shaley loam; but this is of little importance at Limeburners, as nine-tenths of the garden sits on imported soil. Hundreds of tons of top soil were brought in on an endless procession of lorries, so that only one bank to the side of the house consists of the original foundations. The soil was then terraced by machine into a series of flatish areas with gentle slopes between. After building their house at the top of the slope, the owners had the misfortune to choose the drought year of 1976 to make the main planting. I saw the garden about seven years after when it looked wonderful. Today, almost ten years on, with the trees and large shrubs approaching maturity, it can only be described as a knockout.

I hold the view that to be a real success a garden must have a strong motivation or theme. This is why, off the peg gardens rarely succeed. A thorough knowledge of the area, soil, house, surrounds and aspect are vital. Looking at Limeburners, I cannot imagine a better way to have utilized the site.

Great banks of shrub roses mark the entrance from the road. There is a small plantation of lime trees – for the Limehawk Moth – bordered by nepeta, the Catmint, opposite a clipped laurel hedge. One then sees a veritable tour de force: a steep bank of *Hypericum calycinum*, Rose of Sharon, or St John's Wort. This *can* be invasive, but here it covers a difficult situation in a blaze of yellow. When not in flower, the neat oval leaves make inpenetrable ground cover. The whole area is cut with an Alan scythe after flowering, which preserves a uniformly neat appearance. A wonderful example of exactly the right plant growing in the right position.

It is obvious at once that the garden is planned to attract insects. The evocative sound of grasshoppers chirping fills the air, and even early in the year, butterflies abound. We saw a Small Heath, Ringlet and Gatekeeper almost at once. These are all small, brown-coloured butterflies, common on heathland, who lay their eggs on grass. They were on the wing early, as the season was so advanced. The wild meadow was especially sown to provide host plants for butterfly lava, and includes bird's-foot trefoil, horseshoe and kidney vetch, thymes, devil's bit scabious, wood sorrel, ragwort and knapweed. I also saw some tall, blue chicory – *Cichorium intybus* – which must be as beautiful as any cultivated perennial. Needless to say, food plants for butterflies are not neglected, with buddleias (this garden has one of the best collections I have ever seen) sedum, sweet rocket, valarian, scabious and many more simple, nectar producing flowers. In the wilder areas, many of our native shrubs and trees are represented: holly, broom, blackthorn, alder, gorse, privet and dogwood.

If I have given the impression that all this garden is semi-wild, nothing could be further from the truth. The basic design revolves around a huge, sloping lawn with a magnificent blue Atlas Cedar – *Cedrus atlantica glauca* – still immature, but beautifully placed. Wide borders around the lawn are filled with a great variety of plants. Little effort has been made to grow material foreign to the area or aspect, the owners wisely knowing the limitations of the site and working within them. I also admired the way they had planted in large groups. It is a great temptation in a small garden to grow one of

The pool at Limeburners contrasts foliage shapes and colours.

everything in a desperate effort not to miss out a favourite plant. The owners of Limeburners are fortunate in having the space always to plant in a group (I never saw less than three, usually more) and it shows in the planning of the borders.

At the bottom of the sloping lawn is a large pond. I cannot pay a greater compliment to the makers, than to say I had to ask if it were natural. It was not. A butyl lining was used, kept filled for most of the year by an ingenious system of pipes which channel the rainwater from the house further up the slope. The planting of the pond is as well thought out as the method of filling it. The colour is wonderful, but it was the contrast in leaf shape that really took my eye: huge leaves of gunnera, against feathery, *Acer palmatum* 'Dissectum' in green, bronze and purple; arching, narrow grasses with stiff, wide, jagged-edged cardoon.

One of the owners has a degree in horticulture from Studley College and worked in Holland for a year, which must have been a tremendous advantage when planning and planting up the garden.

I must mention one or two real rarities, including a weeping mulberry – *Morus alba* 'Pendula', a very striking, small weeping tree, which is carefully wrapped each winter to protect it from the elements and a well-grown group of *Hydrangea villosa* in a wide border. This not very well known shrub is one of the best of the late flowering hydrangeas. It has a spreading habit with large, flat, mauvy-blue flowers and big, hairy leaves. This needs a position where it is sheltered on the sides from late frosts and cutting winds, but also has clear light overhead. At The Limeburners it is frosted occasionally, but looked superb after two mild winters. Lastly, the very unusual *Dodonia viscosa purpurea* from South America. This has lovely narrow, purple-red leaves. The owners admit it hasn't really been tested yet, but are hopeful.

A final finale from this lovely garden. The owners patronised a young sculptor who crafted both an original and striking piece of work for the garden. Made of stone, brick and wood, it symbolises the spirit of the Industrial Revolution and its later decay at Ironbridge. Backed by a small forest of hebe the owners brought back from the Scilly Isles, their mauve flowers shading to white, and narrow, evergrey-green leaves forming a perfect background, it is yet another example of the thought and planning which have gone into the creation of this superb garden.

Linley Hall ❀ Bishop's Castle

An archetypal English pleasure garden, of parkland, lake, trees and flowers surrounding a perfect Palladian house. Open under the N.G.S., see Yellow Book.

At Linley Hall it is difficult not to be seduced away from contemplation of the gardens to gaze at the house. It was built in 1742 by Henry Joynes of London, surveyor of Kensington Palace and Clerk of the Works to Vanburgh, the builder of Blenheim Palace.

The house, constructed in dressed Grinshill stone of a gorgeously, muted, golden-grey tone, is sited on a slight rise looking over rolling Shropshire hills and a small lake. Anything less like Blenheim couldn't be imagined, as the house is a model of symmetry and simplicity, as well as being of only moderate size. One knows that it is placed in an artificial landscape within formal enclosures (water, walls, trees and a ha-ha) but every facet works so well, looks so natural, one gets the impression that not a tree or urn could be moved without spoiling the overall picture.

Colourful urns on a dull day at Linley Hall.

Each facade of the house is slightly different and acts as the focus of a four sided composition. The east side looks over the lake to a small temple, which has an interesting history. It was once an ice house, used in the days before refrigeration to store in the cold darkness, great blocks of ice cut from the lake. Pillars rescued from a demolished Queen Anne house were utilised to give a Grecian air, and it now makes a wonderful focal point across the water.

The front of the house has an Ionic porch and pedimented windows, which give magnificent uninterrupted views over the ha-ha to typical Shropshire scenery, of low hills and chequer-board fields. Grey urns, in a similar stone to the house, mark the terrace, and are planted up with pink, blue and white petunias, lobelia and geraniums – a lovely contrast against the stone.

The rear portion of the house leads onto a wide lawn and a pretty rose garden. It is cut out of the surrounding trees and backs up against a tall hedge, with a huge statue of Hercules. Smaller lead statues of cherubs and a nymph form a centre piece. The weathered lead (though the statues are modern) again contrasting well with the apricot florabunda rose, 'Wishing'.

Linley Hall's lead nymphs and cherubs.

A long, curving herbaceous border, with a central sundial was full of colour when we visited in late July. Phlox, golden rod and various campanulas made a bright display against a background hedge.

To the right of the house – and almost as large – is a stone stable block, topped by a cupola. This is the same marvellous colour as the house, but made of rough, undressed stone. At the rear (handily placed for manure) is a well-tended vegetable garden. It does not have the classic, high brick walls, but low stone walls and a beech hedge. There are mown grass paths and flowers for cutting – sweet peas and eucalyptus – as well as all the traditional vegetables. The walls of the house are kept pristinely clear of any plant growth, but the stable walls provide shelter and support for red and pink roses.

Scent fills the air, not only from a great bank of lavender outside the stable block, but also the wet, woody smell associated with close, surrounding trees. The trees are a very important part of the garden scene at Linley Hall and include fine larches, which were reputedly planted in about 1750, making them some of the first in the country.

There is a story that they came from the Duke of Atholl's estate in Scotland, whose gardener threw them out when they refused to grow!

Also superb are the oaks. There is a huge tree opposite the stable block, as well as many more in the neighbouring woods. Shropshire was of course once fifty per cent forest, as can be attested by the numerous timber-framed houses. They have, however, gradually been eroded by clearance, until one can only see remnants incorporated into parks around great country houses.

A walk winds alongside the lake of crystal clear water with a long vista to further trees, inviting you to follow it right round to the temple. The vibrations of fish and broken reflections give life and sparkle to the scene even on a dull day, making one realise what an asset such an expanse of water is to a garden.

Linley Hall must be one of the most handsome country houses in the county, its setting, parkland and general ambience quite unforgettable.

Llanyfelin House ❀ Dudleston

A largish garden on a hilly site, illustrating good use of ground cover. Open under the N.G.S., see Yellow Book.

The house is the nucleus of a private garden, and at Llanyfelin it would be difficult to miss. Standing at the top of what can only be described as a *very* steep hill, the Victorian Gothic cottage dominates the garden. Faced with this hill and not wishing formally to terrace, the owners opted for the only possible alternative – ground cover. There is a small flatish area close to the house, part of which is lawn and part given over to a herb garden and a thriving vegetable plot, but four-fifths of the garden is natural, semi-wild terrain planted with a wide variety of trouble free shrubs and perennials, all doing extremely well in the difficult situation.

Wisely, the owners have not confined themselves to low growing material, but have also utilized shrubs as ground cover and some of these are a considerable size. This breaks up the flat areas giving vertical interest to counterbalance the horizontal. Some tension is necessary in the composition of a garden, at Llanyfelin House the balance seems just right. It could be monotonous but isn't, proving that a great deal of thought has gone into the superficially natural atmosphere.

The reason most people give for opting for ground cover is suppression of weeds. This happens up to a point, but it is important to get rid of perennial weeds first, otherwise your ground cover will soon be taken over by the very weeds you hoped to squeeze out. The owners of Llanyfelin also pointed out that one must think further than the flowers when choosing ground cover. In fact, the leaves are pre-eminent, as they will give you the all-season interest which is so vital for success. For this reason, leaf size, colour and texture must be taken into account when planting.

On the steepest part of the slope, prostrate junipers are used to give a dark green, evergreen background, on which the gabled, red-brick house seems to float. To carry on the shrub theme, tough roses such as 'Nevada', 'Paulii', 'Paulii Rosea', 'Raubritter' and the wichuraiana rose thrive in the heavy soil. They grow strongly and are very little pruned. 'Raubritter' is unusual in that its deep pink blooms are cupped into perfect globes. Wichuraiana is very vigorous, sending out long, trailing stems which root as they go. It has lovely dark green, shiny leaves, white scented flowers and little red hips. Another big shrub used is elder in all its many forms: *Sambucus racemosa* 'Plumosa Aurea', as well as *S. nigra* 'Aureomarginata' with yellow edged leaves and 'Laciniata', Fern-leaved Elder, with finely divided leaves. Elder is a much underrated plant for large gardens, and I would also recommend 'Purpurea', with dark purple leaves and pink flowers: an exquisite contrast. All the above can be pruned hard like a buddleia in early spring to make them more acceptable in a smaller area.

Hydrangea petiolaris is a climber, but at Llanyfelin it is successfully used as ground cover, as is variegated ivy, though no attempt is made to prevent them climbing where they will. I also noticed a lovely group of *Viburnum davidii*, with strong, dark-green, corrugated leaves, and – if you have male and female plants – turquoise-blue berries in the autumn.

Juniperus *'Pfitzeriana' making excellent ground cover, Llanyfelin House.*

This seems a good point to emphasise that you nearly always have to plant ground cover in fairly largish groups to get the full impact. The owners have opted for big areas of one plant and *not* fallen into the trap of dotting around several different species or varieties.

If I have given the impression that only common or easy plants are grown, I must list three superb trees all doing well: *Cercidiphyllum japonicum*, a beautiful tree from Japan similar to the Judas Tree, with good autumn colour and caramel scented flowers; the variegated Tulip Tree – *Liriodendron tulipifera* 'Aureomarginatum', with its strange shaped leaves like nothing else in the garden and *Cornus kousa chinensis*. The latter has greeny-white flowers, or rather bracts, poised on the spreading branches like butterflies about to take off.

To return to the ground cover, the first plants that took my eye were the numerous hardy geraniums. I think nearly every form that is easily obtainable is represented, and the owners pick up new sorts whenever they can. It is the ideal easy to grow trouble free plant. It is beautiful in flower, immune to disease, needing no staking, seeding about but never invasively – what more can I say? They are also obtainable in every shade except yellow, so that they fit in with most colour schemes. Hypericum supplies the yellow in the shape of St. John's Wort. Watch this one. It is something of a thug, as is *Lamium galeobdolon* growing nearby. The latter is very pretty with its marbled leaves, but should only be planted in large areas, or where it can be controlled under trees.

Rather more choice perennials used in the shadier parts of the garden are Solomon's Seal and various forms of hellebore, of which *H. orientalis* and *foetidus* are the most successful as the glossy, dark green leaves are evergreen.

There is a boggy area at the bottom of the slope, and once again the owners have decided to go along with the garden, not fighting the natural conditions, but choosing plants which enjoy the damp. I admired the ligularias, 'Desdemona', with round bronze leaves and bright orange daisy flowers and *L. stenocephale* 'The Rocket', with cut leaves and tall, lupin-like blooms. These are both big plants.

Hostas are another good choice for a damp area, increasing in size, beauty and ground covering capability every year. They are completely trouble free unless you have slugs. Believe me, no weed can compete with a well established clump of hosta.

Some might consider this a lazy garden, but with a large, undulating area, both owners working full time, no outside help and a fair amount of work in the vegetable garden alone, it seems to me an ideal solution to the eternal problem of not enough time.

Longnor Hall ❀ near Shrewsbury

A classic seventeenth century house, with extensive deer park and superb trees. Open under the N.G.S., see Yellow Book.

Longnor Hall is a house with both a past and a future. The main building has not been neglected in any serious way, but parts of the large park and garden are in the process of reclamation. The gardener has plans for a water garden herbaceous borders and shrubs, divided from the park by a deep ditch or ha-ha, in what was once part of the cultivated garden and is now little more than a damp wood.

All the ingredients which make up the perfect English country house scene are present at Longnor: the lovely setting with views to The Lawley and Caer Caradoc hills;

Wrought iron tracery, Longnor Hall.

a forty-five acre park with herd of deer; meandering stream (Cound Brook) avenue of noble limes and well placed groups of native trees, all mature and magnificent. Close to the river are two black poplars which are respectively the tallest and the widest in Britain. The girth record of one is 24 feet and the height of the other 124 feet. As both have reached a venerable old age, new ones have been planted nearby to take over this role in the future.

All the many buildings close to the house blend beautifully, from the stable block to the gardener's cottage. Over the river and next to the village a tiny thirteenth century, early English church tops a gentle rise. It is simply built, nave and chancel are one, with a timber belfry and later, old fashioned box pews.

The house itself was built by Sir Richard Corbett in 1670 of red brick. The same red brick, beautifully mellowed by the passing years, is also used in all the walls and outbuildings, a perfect background for plants. The main entrance to the house, with imposing

Attractive pool, Longnor Hall.

steps and Ionic columns, overlooks a flat lawn now grazed by sheep and dotted with superb cedars. I much preferred the south facing garden entrance. Here a well-clipped hedge of beech and yew divides the semi-circular lawn from the park. It is pierced in the centre by a wrought iron gate and bordered with tall columns set into the body of the hedge, each topped by a stone urn: perfect symmetry, visually very satisfying, that echoes the formality of the house; no flowers, just the tranquil beauty of many shades of green.

A wide avenue of grass bordered by clipped yew hedges runs east towards the church. The cultivated garden is on the western side of the house.

Here is the large walled kitchen garden, reminding us what a problem it must have been feeding such a vast household many years ago. The walls are still used for peaches and loganberries, cherries and espalier pears. Apple trees grow in oblong beds, but are severely pruned to keep them within bounds. Moving towards the house, one comes upon a small, enclosed garden with sweet scented lilacs and a deep, stone-edged pond. The proposed new garden leads off from this section. The closer one gets to the house, the more formal the aspect becomes.

First there is an oblong garden bordered by a row of cottages and a tall yew hedge. Tulips and roses bloom close to the brickwork. The fact that it enjoys an unusually sheltered aspect is emphasised by a tender acacia or Wattle, possibly *A. longifolia*, which is one of the hardiest species. It has curious spines, a wonderful, deeply cut, patterned bark, and must be the survivor of many severe winters.

Passing through another beautiful wrought iron gate, one is now in a cultivated area with twin herbaceous borders only recently reclaimed and replanted with phlox, onopordon – the giant thistle, as well as many other old-fashioned perennials and biennials. The grass paths and borders give way to a paved area close to the house.

There is still much work to be done to restore the gardens to their former glory, but the potential is enormous to create a setting worthy of such a glorious house.

Lower Hall ❀ Worfield

Four acres of superb garden, encompassing elegant formality close to the house, and one of the best water gardens in the county. Open under the N.G.S., see Yellow Book.

Lower Hall is a delightful, timber-framed building, dating from the sixteenth century. It is placed in the centre of the village of Worfield, close to the church on the edge of the River Worfe. The buildings and the river dictate the design of the large garden, which falls into two distinct parts. A formal area of separate square or oblong gardens close to the house, and a semi-wild, natural garden alongside the river, with sinuous curves, island beds and smaller streams following the meanders of the water.

The area near the house reminds one strongly of Hidcote (the gardens within a garden idea). The whole of the semi-wild garden is original. The garden designer and writer Lanning Roper had a hand in the original concept, but the owners have adapted and revised his plans, accumulating ideas from garden visits, shows and other sources.

This is a garden of water: channelled and tamed into bubbling fountains close to the house, sliding smoothly by or rushing over the weir on the not inconsiderably sized River Worfe. The sound of water follows you around the garden, while the muffled

Lower Hall, Worfield, a fine example of garden design by Lanning Roper.

Foliage gardening at its very best for colour and contrast.

thump of the Ram pump reminds you that it works continually to feed the fountains and channels.

Plants close to the house benefit from the numerous walls. Mostly built of weathered sandstone, they are the best possible backdrop for the herbaceous perennials, shrubs and roses which spill out of the formal, straight-edged beds: profuse planting in a firm framework. In my opinion this is the only way to treat a formal garden where the basic design is dictated by a square house and boundary wall.

The brick paths, statues, urns and fountains in this part of the garden are quite superb. Most are traditional, as befits the garden of a sixteenth century house, but I noticed one very interesting piece of circular, modern sculpture by Tony Twentyman, based on a mill stone. It did not look in the least out of place because of careful siting near the river.

A picture I shall always remember – white cast iron urns filled with white petunias and geraniums, and the foliage of *Helichrysum petiolatum* backed by a pergola hung with the vine, *Vitis* 'Brant': this, close to a white-grey border containing cardoons, white lavender, a white variegated potentilla, white fox gloves and campanula; also the roses 'Iceberg' (that wonderful floribunda that goes on forever) and the newer 'White Wings', huge single flowers with quite indescribable purple-brown-red anthers.

A red, pink and purple border was another reminder of Hidcote. Here indigofera was in full flower; also pink lavender and a stachys, probably *macrantha*, with stubby, pink flowers, similar to a polygonum.

*Perfectly placed ornaments,
Lower Hall.*

Two formal, square gardens, each with a central water feature form an axis on two sides of the house. One with brick paving and a square pond is surrounded by clipped box and that superb, single rugosa – 'Fra Dagmar Hastrup'. Tiny, pointed pyramids of box emphasise the symmetrical design. The other garden has a larger, more elaborate fountain, and is encircled by an ancient, clipped yew hedge, threaded with the Flame Flower – *Tropaeolum speciosum*.

The whole of the narrow border which divides the garden from the village contains a spectacular collection of hollyhocks – *Althaea rosea*. One rarely sees these typical cottage garden plants as they are a martyr to rust. I have never seen them better grown, though the owner states that they do fall victim to the dreaded plague, when she simply roots them out and plants afresh. There is nothing quite like them for subtle, soft colour in late July when the garden enters a fallow period.

One is very aware that one is in the centre of the village in this part of the garden, in spite of the high wall. Fortunately, the houses around are as aesthetically pleasing as Lower Hall itself, while the large, medieval church of St. Peter is an architectural gem in its own right. An old orchard with mature trees adds to the rural ambience, especially as it contains shrub roses, orange blossom and lilac: food and flowers in authentic cottage style. More old-fashioned blooms fill the beds furthest away from the house – hardy geranium, *Alchemilla mollis*, buddleias and yet more roses. The whole garden is filled with roses, used in every conceivable way from the formal group to the wildest rambler; great swathes of vigorous climbers like 'Bobby James' or 'Seagull' climbing up trees. The high walls make the best of all hosts for roses, but I also counted innumerable honeysuckles and a beautiful specimen of *Ceanothus* 'Gloire de Versailles'. The latter's pale blue, feathery flowers a lovely contrast against the stone. This ceanothus is deciduous and very hardy, but I find it splits badly when grown as a free standing shrub. It needs the firm support of a stake or a wall to prevent the weight of flower literally pulling it apart. There is a delightful pink form called 'Pink Perle' which is equally good.

After walking across a wide lawn which separates the formal garden and house from the river, one crosses a bridge and enters another world. There are in fact several bridges – the water garden is vast. One was built by P.O.W. labour just after the war. Not all of the ground is swampy. A well-drained river walk has been planted with a selection of trees, most of which, while enjoying a deep moist soil, do not appreciate wet. The large island beds in this part of the garden are a complete contrast to the severe angles so in keeping with the house, not a straight line in sight!

Of course there are disadvantages in having such a large, powerful river so close; not the least being the odd dead sheep floating past and occasional flooding. The semi-wild bank was once planted up with rhodo-dendrons (one side of the river is acid, the other alkaline) but the river flooded badly in 1982, then froze solid, effectively ruining the whole planting.

It is impossible to pick out more than a few of the more interesting trees. One completely new to me was

Hollyhocks 'Alcea Rosea'.

Magnolia obovata, with huge, oval leaves. It has creamy-white, fruit-salad scented flowers in June, with striking, crimson stamens. Most of the ornamental trees were planted about fifteen to twenty years ago, only a group of huge alders being there already. This was hard to believe when I stood under a giant poplar, *Populus* 'Robusta', towering above my head. How wise to put a river between it and the house. There was a lovely group of the river birch, with tattered, brown bark, as well as *Betula costata* with the usual white bark and good, yellow, autumn colour. *B. jacquemontii*, I do know well, it has the most dazzling, white trunk of all the birches. *B. albo-sinensis*, from China as its name indicates, has an incredible pinky-red bark – very unusual. I must also mention a rare conifer – *Sciadopitys verticillata*, the Japanese Umbrella Pine, with clusters of shiny green needles and round, fat cones like solid, half-open roses. (This must be a gift to the dried flower addicts.) At the end of this river walk, which gradually becomes wilder the further you are from the house, are groups of trees grown for their ornamental bark. *Prunus serrula, Acer davidii* – The Snake Bark Maple, and many more. A final choice to describe – *Aesculus* × *mutabilis* 'Induta', a shrimp-pink, flowering member of the Horse Chestnut family. There is a definite American tinge to the underplanting in this area – trilliums and pachistina.

There are many good gardens in Shropshire, but Lower Hall must take its place among the very best for its superb collection of plants, sympathetic development of the site, and faultless taste in garden ornaments.

The Lyth ❀ near Ellesmere

A four acre garden set in beautiful parkland, noted for its mature rhododendrons and azaleas. Open under the N.G.S., see Yellow Book.

The garden at The Lyth is dominated by the house it surrounds. Fortunately, the latter is architecturally eminent: a perfect Regency colonial gem in cream stucco, with a pretty trellis veranda in cast iron, very typical of the period and almost certainly cast at Coalbrookdale. The owner thinks that it may have been floated by barge from its original place of manufacture to the nearby canal wharf in Ellesmere.

The main garden front faces south, with views across an undulating lawn over rolling, hilly parkland so distinctive of this part of Shropshire. The glaciers of the last Ice Age leaving, not only the remains of lakes, but also drumlins: i.e. miniature hills of many different types of soil, carried long distances by the rivers of ice and left wherever they melted. It is the fate of The Lyth to rest on a free draining mound of acid, sandy loam. This causes tremendous problems in dry weather. The owners still mention the drought years of the mid-seventies with great feeling.

So often a garden of this type, though elaborately laid out in Victorian times, is left in the twentieth century with nothing more than the remnants of its former glory – a few fine trees and a sprinkling of rhododendrons. Rhododendrons and fine trees there certainly are in plenty at The Lyth, the blaze of colour from the large mature bushes rising high above tall walls and big trees, but this is far from all. The Lyth is fortunate in having an owner who takes an active interest in the layout, maintenance and variety of plants in the grounds. The south lawn has several island beds, one consisting almost entirely of heathers (which are also ideally suited to the sandy loam) and including a tree heather. Another holds a great variety of choice

Sandy soil at The Lyth suits heathers, brooms and conifers.

herbaceous perennials. Beds closer to the parkland contain fascinating small trees: especially a group of mature acers with sculpted stems dating from the turn of the century when they formed part of a sunken Japanese garden. Specimen azaleas dot this lawn. Some are examples of the original species used in the production of the Ghent Hybrids in Belgium between 1830 and 1850. They have long-tubed very fragrant flowers, and come into bloom later, about the end of May. *Rhododendron ponticum*, which infests the peaty woods round the meres close by, has to be kept under close watch and regularly cut back to prevent it overwhelming the more choice stock; though I found the great dark mounds of mauve and green a delightful contrast to the square, pale house.

All the great, classic trees are represented: copper beech, cedars, yews and oaks. Of greater interest to me were some immense variegated hollies, clipped into tall columns every winter to supply berries for the house. Also a very large example of the local Dovastoniana yew, with dark, pendulous branches, grown from the original tree which still exists in the nearby village of West Felton.

On the western side of the house lies the vast, walled, vegetable garden. This used to supply the needs of the whole household, fully employing the labour of a man with three boys to help him. Once overgrown, it is now beautifully laid out with neat rows of vegetables, the walls utilized for early plums and the self fertile cherries Stella and Morello. The garden side of the great wall is not wasted, forming a backdrop for a wide shrub and herbaceous border, containing a host of good plants: Ceanothus, the climbing rose, *ecae*, superficially very like the better known *R.* 'Canary Bird', with single flowers of deep, buttercup yellow, *Cytisus battandieri*, with its exquisite silvery leaves and pineapple scented yellow flowers – this one *must* have a warm wall – as well as the more common lilac and weigela.

An historical footnote: The Lyth is the birthplace of Eglantyne Jebb, founder of Save the Children.

Mallards Keep ❀ Church Stretton

A tiny garden in a quiet street, packed to bursting with peat-loving plants. Open under the N.G.S., see Yellow Book.

The garden at Mallards Keep is living proof that even if your garden is small, your ideas certainly don't have to be. An ordinary, rather pleasant, well-tended suburban garden you might think after a cursory glance over the low wall from the pavement outside. Nothing could be further from the truth. Suburban certainly, but there is little ordinary about this garden. The rear area is a revelation in how successful something so different can be when carried out with sufficient confidence and aplomb; provided of course, you also have a sure knowledge of the ultimate height and spread of the plants used.

Many of the larger acers are carefully pruned to fit in; the *Acer micranthum* can only be described as pollarded. I certainly never realised that this kind of treatment could be so successful, though I had seen examples from Japan where pines are sometimes pruned needle by needle to obtain absolutely the right spread and shape.

The owners of Mallards Keep have gardened on the thin, shaley, acid soil for over twenty years, gradually adding plants until the garden is literally bursting at the seams with the beautiful and unusual. Three stone troughs near the house are planted with small, cushion-forming alpines, as interesting out of flower as when covered in blooms. These the owner covers with perspex in the winter to keep off the damp, an enemy of many alpines, rather than to protect against cold.

The ground is too badly drained for most rock plants, so a raised scree bed has been constructed to grow such treasures as *Polygala chamaebuxus* 'Rhodopetera', which in a mild season will flower all winter. The house walls have been utilized to support the *Ceanothus* 'Italian Skies' superficially very similar to the common *C.* 'Delight', but the blue of its flowers is a particularly intense shade.

Rosa banksiae 'Lutea' also grows on the same wall, a somewhat rampant rose for a small house, especially as it flowers on second and third year old wood, so resents heavy pruning. But who would be without it if there is the slightest chance of persuading it to flower? Each yellow bunch of tiny, double flowers a Victorian posy in its own right. It won't die on you in any but the most severe winter, but you must give it a position where the shoots will ripen to bloom successfully.

Hebes are always tricky, even when you don't live seven hundred feet above sea level, but the tender *H. hulkeana* was doing well in a border close to the house. I suspect this hebe is a good deal hardier than we are led to believe. The form grown at Mallards Keep is × *fairfieldii*, which is dwarfer and hardier than the type. If you have

The tiny garden at the rear of Mallards Keep.

never tried hulkeana, get one. The large panicles of lavender-blue flowers are nothing like any other hebe, much larger and more open – definitely worth a place in the sun.

As the garden is barely a sixth of an acre, I don't think I would be believed if I gave a list of the rhododendrons growing at the rear of the house. Sufficient to say that the collection covers most types, including one of the biggest and best yakushimanum I have ever seen. All the latter, species and newer hybrids, are perfect rhododendrons for a small garden, being hardy, compact and as beautiful in leaf as in flower. It is not to be missed if you garden on acid soil, the leaves with their brown-tomentose underneath look wonderful all year, unlike so many hybrids. The type plant, with dark-pink buds fading to pale-pink and later white, has yet to be bettered in my opinion.

Somehow, the owners have also found room for many shade loving herbaceous plants: dog-tooth violets – *Erythronium dens-canis*, daffodils and more than twenty clematis.

I was especially impressed by a pink *Clematis alpina*, 'Willy', a lovely contrast to the more common blue, 'Frances Rivis'.

Two memories to carry away are of a large *Acer palmatum* 'Chitoseyama', underplanted with blue rhododendron in every tint from mauve to pale, clear azure, and including, 'Blue Tit', 'Augfast', 'Blue Diamond', augustinii, and 'Blue Mist' and at their feet, *Iris innominata*, a fabulous warm yellow, veined and marked with bronze: only a few flowers, but what a wonderful sight.

Merton Nursery Garden ✿ Bicton, near Shrewsbury

A medium sized garden noted for its impressive collection of conifers. Nursery and garden open most weeks of the year, including Sunday, 9-6 pm.

Visitors to the North Wales coast rushing along the busy A5 main road on the outskirts of Shrewsbury pass a sign with Merton Nursery in green on gold. Nothing unusual you may think, after all there are at least six garden centres on the A5 by-pass, but this one is very special by virtue of the superb garden behind it. The whole nursery and garden have been created over the last twenty years from a rough field and small wood by the owner and his brother. Although he now has help in the nursery the owner still maintains the garden practically on his own.

A special feature of the garden is the wonderful collection of conifers, over eighty varieties, all planted since 1961. The vast majority are dwarf forms, but some have grown to a good size and give this comparatively new garden a settled air. The soil is an excellent free-draining loam, very fertile, and obviously suits the conifers.

Yews and junipers seem to be the owner's special favourites, and he has them in every possible colour and shape. I particularly admired *Taxus baccata* 'Dovastonii', a yew with wide spreading pendulous branches, which, strangely enough, was first discovered at West Felton, a village only a little further along the A5.

I love the blue spruce, *Picea pungens* 'Koster', a marvellous duck-egg blue. But an even better one grows here, *Picea p.* 'Thomsen', a striking silver-blue. Both these make superb lawn specimens.

There are so many junipers, I hardly know where to begin. They vary in size from a tall pair of *Juniperus communis glauca* marking the end of the lawn where a path leads to the wood, down to such miniatures as *Juniperus communis* 'Compressa', *the* perfect rock garden conifer. In the centre of the beautifully tended lawn is a huge specimen of *Juniperus × media* 'Pfizeriana Aurea', and just the right distance away, a blue Mount Atlas Cedar. The tongue-twister pfizeriana is, of course, many inexperienced gardeners' idea of a perfect rock garden conifer. How wrong can you be: it looks so innocent in its little plastic container. Then, before you can say pfitzeriana – if you can say it that is – the whole rock garden has disappeared, never mind your *Juniperus* 'Compressa'. But the owner of this garden has never erred. The dreaded pfitzeriana has a place of honour which it richly deserves in the main lawn, where one can walk all round it admiring its unique habit of growth.

The design of this garden falls into three distinct parts: herbaceous borders, lawn with conifers, sun-loving shrubs and rockery, backed by the woodland garden with specimen deciduous trees and shade-loving plants.

The main herbaceous border runs the full length of the road which leads to the nursery. It tends to be at its best in late summer and contains some annuals, biennials and shrubs specially placed to fill the gaps left by early flowers. In such a large border the owner can afford to grow the plants in really generous clumps, which makes it very effective indeed. My particular favourites include acanthus, sedums, phlox, helianthus, geums, nepeta, and, less usual in an herbaceous border, Pampas grass. I also loved the sweet william, yuccas and some of the biggest clumps of lavender I have ever seen. The background to this border is mostly provided by conifers clipped hard. At the lower end the owner was experimenting with a hedge of *Cedrus atlantica glauca*. At today's prices you really would have to own a nursery to try this.

Contrasting conifers at Merton.

Most of the specimen conifers are grouped around the lawn and rockery at the back of the house, where they enjoy full sun and are sheltered by the small wood. A number of the shrubs grown with them are evergreen or ever-grey, and their rounded shape contrasts with the strong upward thrust of the conifers.

Behind the lawn are the island beds which house perennial and foliage plants. Shrub and conifer edged paths lead you into the small wood. It is very damp underfoot; ideal for the moisture loving rhododendrons and azaleas thriving under a canopy of silver birch and acers. This is almost a wild garden, with an abundance of self-seeding foxgloves; although it is all so beautifully cared for, that the description seems singularly inappropriate.

Here also flourish a varied collection of the now very fashionable hostas, a plant which really appreciates the damp shade, never growing to their luxuriant best in hot, dry conditions. Even the giant foliage plant *Gunnera manicata* grows well, showing how damp the ground must be.

All the everyday paraphernalia of a nursery are screened from the garden by tall conifers. The vegetable garden too, although huge – the nursery was once a market garden – is not obtrusive.

The owner welcomes garden enthusiasts whenever the nursery is open. And, at whatever time of the year you decide to visit, the many conifers help to create that rarest of phenomena, a garden at its best all the year round.

Millichope Park ❀ Munslow

Thirteen acres of Romantic, landscape garden, comprising lake, temple and magnificent trees, overlooked by an architecturally distinguished neo-classical house. Open under the N.G.S., see Yellow Book.

The landscape garden at Millichope Park revolves around the lake and columned rotunda or temple. The water is a calm reflecting mirror, centred in a green circle of grass and trees.

The garden was laid out in the early nineteenth century, and is dominated by the great sandstone house, with its row of huge, Ionic columns facing the sweep of lawn leading down to the lake. It was built in 1840, but looks much older than an early Victorian house. The round temple which sits perfectly on a natural dam of deeply cut sandstone, and whose columns echo those of the house, is older, dating from about 1785. One cannot help feeling that the house was influenced by the temple, rather than the other way round!

This is an all year round garden, but we chose to visit on a still, misty, autumnal day, when the great trees, for which the garden is renowned, were at their colourful best. Copper beeches, in a exquisite pale-orange shade, dip their branches into the lake, while another had turned to a dull alizarin crimson, providing a lovely background for a grey-green shepherdess on the terrace. Her shepherd companion, was backed by the yellow-brown leaves of the common beech. Rich, dark green is provided by the mighty conifers on the sloping lawn; some are the largest of their kind in Shropshire.

They include a Lawson's Cypress – *Chamaecyparis lawsoniana*, usually seen as a tortured hedge round suburban houses, but at Millichope, seeming to stretch to the sky as the mist engulfed it. It is I believe, over a hundred and ten feet tall. There are also two Douglas Firs, *Pseudotsuga menziesii*, an *Abies procera*, Noble Fir and a sequoia, Californian Redwood, with reddish-brown, spongy bark, all well over a hundred feet.

The temple stands in the shade of a spectacular cedar of Lebanon 125 feet high. So often when they reach this size, branches are blown away, or break under the weight of heavy snow. At Millichope, the tree is beautifully balanced, so that the strong horizontal growth, contrasts with the upright columns at its feet. A bright-red vine, *Vitis coignetiae*, has casually draped itself like a scarf around the trees and bushes near the base of the temple; sweeping, graceful, swags, set against tight, sculptured formality – absolutely perfect.

The park is a natural haven for wild life. Swans with an extended family of cygnets buried their heads in the lake; Canada geese grazed the lawn; the garden right up to the formal terrace was alive with female pheasants: some balancing on the low wall, others pecking hopefully under trees and shrubs. A large posse of squirrels, helping themselves to a bumper harvest of sweet chesnuts, ran for their lives up the steps to the higher terrace as we approached. The peeps of a coot, and the splashing as it trod water were very loud in the still air, thrown back by the high sandstone wall on which sits the temple, and the surrounding amphitheatre of grass.

From 1939 until the early sixties the house was used as a school, only returning to the hands of the present owners some twenty years ago. The grounds were neglected during this period, needing a programme of replanting and renovation to bring them back to something like their former glory. The aim was to create in a large area, a practical, but typical garden, sympathetic to the house its setting and the life-style of the present occupants. To this end, rhododendrons and bulbs provide colour and interest in spring, together with wild flowers in the damp, grassed area beyond the lake. Summer sees the herbaceous borders blooming, and autumn brings perhaps the most fascinating season of all, when the trees are at their vibrant best.

Contrary to general opinion, wild gardens are *not* a soft option, being difficult to plant and maintain. At Millichope, rabbits are an additional hazard when attempting to

A tranquil autumn day in Millichope Park.

establish desirable native flora. The owners are forced to encircle newly planted areas with wire rings until the roots are settled, or voracious rabbits dig everything up. Grass too, must be left until leaves die or seeds ripen, but mown paths help to create some order until the main cut can commence.

The herbaceous garden consists of a series of small gardens, sheltered by the terrace wall and clipped yew hedges. One contains matching, oblong ponds with gold-fish and water lilies; pink nerines thriving in the narrow border. Further along grow indigofera, clematis, abutilon and a very good form of *Hedera helix* 'Sagittifolia', with a long, central lobe. The second enclosed square garden has the corners cut and curved to accommodate more herbaceous perennials and small trouble-free shrubs, such as spiraea, potentilla and Tree Mallow. A superb lead trough filled with *Helichrysum petiolatum* in gold and grey-green faces a stone seat set against the terrace wall. The last garden neatly conceals the swimming pool from the view beneath its rose-hung walls.

Millichope Park.

The lake is artificial, and was created by damming a steam which eventually runs into the River Corve. There is a woodland walk along the upper valley, following the course of the stream and a series of silting pools. Behind the house, I noted another long herbaceous border against a retaining wall, topped by an orchard which must be a picture in springtime: blossom on a level with the windows!

There are so many perfect touches, blending the natural with the contrived: a multi-coloured island in the lake-acers and rhododendron foliage, yew berries, translucent red against the darkest

Copper beech in autumn dress.

green, ivy and wild strawberry leaves in the stone terrace steps, beautiful urns again filled with *Helichrysum petiolatum* and variegated ivy, great cream, oval baths, overflowing with nicotiana. The ornaments and sculpture deserve a chapter to themselves. The urns are contemporary with the house, though the shepherd and shepherdess who look so at home, were a wedding present. In the park, close to the lake, is a delightful otter sculpted by Sally Arnup. Further on a pair of lead greyhounds scent the air as if looking out for those elusive rabbits. Realistic sculpture always works so well in a natural setting in grass or backed by trees. The contorted boles of some of the bigger trees are equally interesting from a sculptural point of view. In this wilder part of the garden are great stands of bulrushes, like dark-brown lances. Further on, a creamy-grey cupid, still inhabits the temple under the cedar.

This was one of the few gardens we did not see in sunshine, but the lack of hard shadows and bright light, rather added to its attractions than detracted from its beauty.

Moortown ❀ near Wellington

A large plantsman's garden, packed with rare and interesting treasures. Open under the N.G.S., see Yellow Book.

As soon as I walked into the garden at Moortown, I was struck by an overwhelming sense of familiarity. Had I been there before? Dreamt a visit even? The owner soon put me onto the right track: he is a friend of the late Margery Fish – her garden at East Lambrook is a place of pilgrimage for all serious gardeners. Moortown contains many of the plants she introduced or returned to favour through her immensely readable books.

You can name on the fingers of one hand the great gardeners who can also write well – Christopher Lloyd, E.A. Bowles, Vita Sackville West, Gertrude Jekyl; but Margery Fish would certainly be there in that select band. As I read and reread all her books on a regular basis, a visit to Moortown is rather like visiting old friends.

The present owner expanded the garden from a small area around the main buildings, utilizing a tennis court and an old orchard; though the dignified red-brick house dates from 1840, and his family have farmed the sur-

Moortown is renowned for its tulip collection.

rounding land for four generations. I heard horror stories about how practically the entire garden was used for growing vegetables during the war and just after. From the mature settled air, and the size of the trees and shrubs, one would never guess that it didn't date from the same time as the house.

The main garden consists of a series of parallel borders with grass walks between, one covered by an iron pergola rescued from a demolished house nearby. There is definitely a Victorian feel to this part of the garden. The owner states that he wishes he had started with a more deliberate plan, but for me it was hard to imagine anything better or more in keeping with the house.

Then there are the plants: where to begin, so many rare and unusual, all beautiful and interesting. The first that took my eye was a golden *Valeriana phu* 'Aurea'. It does apparently become greener as summer approaches, but was a blaze of yellow as bright as any daffodil on the April day I saw it. Another common cottage garden plant, now rarely seen, was *Bellis perennis* 'Dresden China', an exquisite little pink double daisy. I have tried them in my own garden, but find that they *will* hybridize with the daisies in the lawn! Like the double primroses, they need constant division to keep them happy.

There are many herbs in the garden, including several unusual variegated forms; but all are interspersed with other plants rather than occupying a formal herb garden on their own. As many herbs are frankly a leggy, rank pain in the neck by mid-summer, I can only applaud this idea. I also get the impression that the owner grows his herbs for visual effect, rather than the pot. A good tip from my own garden is to cut them down in late spring, encouraging new young growth from the base, so rejuvenating them. A grouping I especially admired were bronze fennel and Bowles Golden Grass, with variegated comfrey. A lovely constrast in both colour and texture, fitting snugly into a corner.

There are many superb narcissus, but I found the square, chequered bells of *Fritillaria meleagris*, the Snakes's Head Fritillary, even more exciting; especially the white form and the extra dark, 'Charon'. *Fritillaria imperialis* was present in force as befits a Victorian garden, but what a thrill to see the rare variegated form flourishing, each narrow leaf outlined in creamy-white. It is a shy beauty, and doesn't flower every year, but when it does, the hanging bells are orange tinted.

Many of the plants at Moortown were completely new to me. After enthusing over a yellow pulmonaria, I was gently set right. It was in fact the biennial, *Nonnea lutea* – amazingly alike.

There is a large bed of mature shrub roses, underplanted with unusual herbaceous perennials. The roses include 'President de Seze', 'Honorine de Brabant', 'Chapeau de Napoleon' – a heavily crested pink moss, the buds covered in fuzz – and the old favourite and utterly reliable rugosa, 'Roseraie de L'Hay'.

Two stone pillars were rescued from the same demolished garden as the iron pergola. One is covered with the golden ivy 'Clouded Gold', the rose, 'Paul's Lemon Pillar', and topped with an urn. Another idea that appealed was a bed given over to plant thugs which are left to fight it out among themselves. At least you get some idea of what you are letting yourself in for with giant hog weed, but what about that super-spreader *Lamium galeobdolon*? So pretty in its little pot, until of course, it takes over the whole garden. The owner tells me the thug bed is shaded by tall trees in the summer, which also inhibits their growth.

Amongst the shrubs, *Rubus spectabilis*, making a rounded bush, not a bramble, was a mass of small, raspberry-pink flowers. In the hedge I noted *Rubus ulmifolius* 'Bellidiflorus', an unusual double form which I have coverted for many years, but never before seen in the flesh. Close by was the elm, 'Jacqueline Hillier', its early growth making neat, parallel rows, all the branches overlapping to form an intriguing tracery. The owner tells me it is the last deciduous tree in the garden to lose its leaves.

The garden boasts a wonderful collection of saddle stones, millstones and troughs from the farmyard. The troughs tightly packed with sempervivums, and all sympathetically arranged to fit in with the layout of the house and garden. I was struck by the rightness of the house setting, natural stone walls, brickwork and close, but unobtrusive, farm buildings. How often a farmyard and garden are spoilt by hideously modern, unimaginatively planned farm buildings.

The garden is open to all the winds that blow, with magnificent views across the plain to the Wrekin: but it does benefit from mature shelter belts of holly and oak.

In the walled kitchen garden are the owner's collection of English tulips, which really merit a chapter to themselves. Sufficient to say that they are very beautiful and *very* difficult to maintain. Fire blight frequently strikes, and the collection is impossible to verify, as it changes year by year as the tulips break into different colours induced by virus disease. It is the virus of course which causes the exotic streaking and mottling.

My favourite flower in this garden of treasures? Not as difficult to name as you might imagine. In a sheltered courtyard at the side of the house the owner grows *Hepatica triloba*, in the rare double form, its small, exquisite, blue flowers appearing as soon as there is a mild spell in early spring.

The Morleys ❀ near Church Stretton

Four acres of sheer delight. One of the best private gardens in Shropshire whether you are expert or amateur. No longer open to the public.

I have visited this garden on three occasions over a period of ten years, and each time, having found it quite perfect, was astonished to discover it even better when I returned. My first impression was of a garden at its peak. Sometimes one gets the idea that a garden needs time for trees to mature, shrubs to spread. Or conversely, that a garden is overblown – trees now shading too large an area, herbaceous perennials too thick on the ground. The Morleys is just right – always. I now realise of course that this does not happen by magic, but by hard work and a constant programme of lifting, up-dating, pruning and re-arranging the material in the garden. I have lost count of the new varieties first seen in this delightful garden. The owner admits to being quite ruthless in her search for new and better forms of perennials and shrubs, leaving no stone unturned in her search when she spots or reads of something she would like.

The owners bought the property thirty-seven years ago, and describe it as a *very* neglected smallholding sitting amidst four acres of weeds. There were no trees excepting an old pear; but there was potential for those with imagination to see it in the gently sloping site, pleasant, grey-fawn sandstone of the buildings, and the delightful, meandering stream close to the front of the house. Less welcome was the soil, a heavy clay; though it does bring a bonus of fertility once worked and mulched.

The basic plan of the garden is of island beds filled with a mixed planting of perennials and shrubs, very much in the style of Burford. The latter garden is much admired by the owners of The Morleys, and was a great influence on both the design and the choice of plant associations. I would in fact describe the garden as a mini-Burford, on a smaller and more intimate scale. There are no fine views, the plants press in close around the house, but there is also very little wind; a point appreciated by the owners, who gladly swop sweeping prospects of distant hills for shelter.

This is yet another garden where it seems easier to list the plants *not* grown. Rarities there are in abundance, but the common is not despised providing it is good of its kind. For example, in an oval, slightly raised bed devoted to alpines and mulched with gravel, I found many old favourites, including the white form of thrift – *Armeria maritima* 'Alba', and the white *Dianthus deltoides* 'Alba', a lovely pure white with dark-red line close to the centre. Like the thrift it is quite as easy and floriferous as its more common pink and red relations; also dwarf hardy geraniums, helianthemums (including some very good double forms which retain their flowers longer) and sempervivums.

A complete contrast is the damp bed alongside. Here spiraeas, *Iris kaempferi*, mimulus and rodgersia grow strongly in the moisture retentive soil.

A group of small trees planted in grass echoes the circular beds; these are underplanted with bulbs, so must stand in rough grass until the leaves die back. The foilage contrasts are lovely: the gold of gleditsia against the blue of a spruce.

Maintenance is superb, everything is grown well, but areas of wild flowers and long grass against hedges and under trees point up the crisp edging and tailored lawn, while avoiding that over-manicured, super-meticulous, unnatural look.

Very large beds in the middle of the sloping lawn contain some wonderful plants, the now mature trees giving a variety of growing conditions from quite deep shade, through dappled light, to full sun. The trees are mostly sorbus, which are just big enough and thick enough for the purpose intended. *Potentilla* 'Red Ace', always tricky as it won't flower in deep shade, but like many other red and pink potentillas fades badly in direct sun, does very well in this bed (the yellows are mostly sun proof); also *Alstroemeria ligtu* and its hybrids. If you cannot grow the latter, try *A.aurantiaca*, a blazing orange, and once established, one of the best perennials for cutting or making a showy patch of

The Morleys is a typical Shropshire stone cottage set in its own gentle valley.

colour in the mid-summer garden. I also admired the blue poppies, *Meconopsis grandis* and × *sheldonii*, two very good varieties (I would also recommend *M.* × *sheldonii* 'Branklyn' which I grow myself) as well as self-sown seedlings in a subtle, shot-silk, mauve-blue. These all need damp, acid soil and light shade to do well.

Allium giganteum give interest in the border.

Conifers add substance to the deciduous shrubs in the beds and give interest in the winter. Their definite shapes, rounds, cones and uprights, as well as the strong green of their foliage, form a good background for the more amorphous yellows and paler greens of *Spiraea* 'Gold Flame', a gorgeous pale-blue hibiscus, and the deeply cut leaves of *Paeonia lutea ludlowii*. The latter, with the tree paeony delavayi, are good to start with if you are inexperienced, as hybrid tree paeonies can be tricky.

The vegetable garden, which is hidden from the house by a hedge, mirrors the lay-out of the flower garden, being island beds set in lawn. In the case of the vegetables however, they are square. Fruit trees grow in grass, inhibiting their size and vigour; a good idea in a small plot.

At this point one thinks that one has seen everything, but, if you walk on a little further through a path at the edge of the vegetables, you come to yet another delightful area of semi-wild garden called by the owners, 'Shep's acre'. This is not because the poor dog is buried there, but because it was his favourite haunt (having spotted several rabbits I now understand why)!

In spite of this all too familiar menace, wide paths of mown grass are bordered by rough grass containing yet more choice shrubs and trees. I will concentrate though on the Burnet roses, *Rosa pimpinellifolia*, which are a feature of this part of the garden and rarely seen en masse nowadays. They are small in every sense: tiny leaves and exquisite, miniature double flowers in shades of pink, yellow, red, white and a quite fabulous mauve. You can also obtain the more common single kind, but for me, the tiny, double blooms, only an inch or so across and borne in profusion, are unique. Only 'Cecile Brunner' or the Threepenny Bit Rose, *R. farreri* 'Persetosa' are in any way similar. They are not easy to obtain. A specialist old rose or shrub rose nursery is your best bet. Alternatively cultivate a friend who grows them, or look out for a society like the National Council for the Conservation of Plants and Gardens, the N.C.C.P.G., devoted to preserving all the old and neglected plants in our gardens.

Nordybank Nurseries ❀ Clee St. Margaret

A medium sized, truly natural garden, set in typical Shropshire hill country. Open in season, when plants from the garden are for sale.

Many gardens described as country or natural are no such thing, merely paying lip service to the idea. True, they may incorporate, typical, cottage garden plants, or aim for a studied informal air, but their hearts are still in suburbia: the owner cannot resist tidying up the edges, religiously hoeing out every weed, or including exotic plants quite at variance with the original conception. Now all this is perfectly alright of course – provided you don't pretend the result is natural! The garden at Nordybank is one of the very few, which really does deserve the epithet.

It covers about an acre of heath-like hillside, halfway up a typical, rounded mound, in the heart of the South Shropshire countryside. It was a wonderful, hot, sunny August day when we visited, and I can honestly say that I have never seen so many butterflies, in such diversity, in my life. They are attracted by all the herbs and wild flowers, many of which are their host plants, but also by the buddleias.

The latter are left completely unpruned, to build up wind resistant, woody frames, covered in sweet-scented, long racemes of blossom. All the common sorts flourish, many are self-seeded; but choicer forms, such as 'Dartmoor', with bushy, many-branched flowers, and a glorious true red, called 'Royal Red', also exist side by side. These buddleias, together with the old shrub roses, make up the backbone of the garden, giving it height and structure.

There is a great deal of natural woodland surrounding the garden, and small pieces, in the form of individual birch, rowan and alder find their way into the garden. The views are spectacular: miles of panoramic, chequer-board fields spread out below. Surprisingly, the garden is not too windy, as it is protected on the east and north by the slope of the hill and the trees.

The house, too, is perfectly in tune with the garden, a low, unspoilt cottage, in red Devonian sandstone. The owner feels very strongly about the suburbanisation of the countryside. The tidying up of the cottage and garden, with coloured cement paving stones, pierced concrete walls, post and chain fences, new windows out of character with the house and area and all the many other tasteless excrescences imported into the countryside to give a totally alien effect. She has tried hard not to tame her hillside too much, but to let nature take its course with only the minimum of interference. At Nordybank, nothing is ever replanted. The owner accepts the hint, if a subject languishes, that it is not right for the garden.

This is essentially a summer garden, though large groups of daffodils and other bulbs have been planted in the rough grass under trees to give early interest.

One of the most fascinating areas for me was a large, square bed at the

Nordybank Nurseries.

top of the slope protected by hedges and devoted to some unusual herbs, used for other than culinary purposes. This was once the cottage vegetable garden, and has extra good soil. Most of the herbs are native wild plants, or ones introduced hundreds of years ago and naturalised. They include some dye plants – *Genista tinctoria*, like a large-flowered broom, a cream verbascum and golden rod, which all give yellow-green tints, also Madder, which produces red. Another lovely herb, which does have a place in the pot, was a white hyssop. I grow the common blue form, which is worthy of a place in any herbaceous border, but I found the white equally delightful.

The most appropriate word I can think of to describe the main planting is blowsy. Everything natural and unrestrained, with no attempt to coerce the plants into any direction other than the one they want to go: great clumps of mallow in every shade of pink, and including our own native Marsh Mallow, holding each other up, or leaning heavily on the roses; Toadflaxes growing through an achillea; tall, blue, double, hardy geraniums propped up against an old stone wall.

The plants are well grouped for colour and size, but there is no pretension to be anything other than a simple, country garden. Incidentally, nothing is cut down until the spring following flowering, so that seeding and protection from frost by top growth, is kept to a maximum. A bonus are the dried flower heads such as teasel, which are excellent as winter decoration.

The owner has lived in the house for nine years, but the main planting only took place about three years ago. Because quick herbaceous plants along with buddleias and roses were used, however, and the trees already existed, the site has a mature feel. There is a natural stone terrace in the same material as the house, where one can sit and enjoy the plants, the view and drink in the heavy scent filling the air, while butterflies flit past in vast numbers. The terrace merges with the garden well, buddleias of great size almost invading the house, which is hung with honeysuckle.

I realise that we saw this garden at the best possible time and on the best possible day, but I loved it, and felt many owners of so called natural gardens could learn a lot from a summer visit.

Oldfield ✹ Craven Arms

A three acre, semi-woodland garden on a sloping site, with extensive views over beautiful countryside. Open under the N.G.S., see Yellow Book.

Oldfield was created not from a single house and garden, but from a small hamlet of no less than seven cottages and four barns, with attendant walls, hedges and outbuildings. All were demolished, with the exception of one great barn which was converted into a comfortable house; though the date from an old farmhouse – 1747 – is incorporated into the terracing wall.

The garden is constructed on the side of a gentle hill, backing up against deciduous woods of native trees, and with far-away views over the South Shropshire countryside. Even that desirable element, water, is present: a tiny rivulet filling a natural pond. It is hard to imagine a more promising site, though the shaley, stoney soil, overlying thick, blue clay, can be both very wet and hungry in places.

Ten years ago, when the owners moved in, the great disadvantages were those of drainage and the thick growth of weeds and scrub. Advantages included an inexhaustible supply of beautifully weathered stone from the demolished cottages and the superb south-westerly aspect. The drainage problem was tackled with pipes laid in trenches, the planting of shrubs and trees which enjoy wet, such as cornus and willow, and terracing.

The rear of the house backs up against the steepest part of the hill, and here most of the stone was utilized in a series of banked low walls. The range of plants on show late in the year included prostrate junipers, excellent for both ground cover and a fresh, green look in mid-winter, potentilla, hardy geranium, vinca at the base of the lowest wall and several extremely floriferous polygonums; *P. affine*, an old favourite, but also a tiny, evergreen version, with oval dark leaves and minute, pale-pink pokers. This was still flowering its heart out in late October.

One looks up the hill in this part of the garden to a densely wooded, gloriously coloured, autumn scene: a perfect backdrop to the terracing. Some trees stood out from the general, greeny-gold tones: Sorbus of course, in brilliant oranges and dull red, *Betula jacque-montii*, with intensely white bark and yellow leaves, and a magnificent amelanchier in glowing red.

The house border holds tender shrubs – *Cytisus battandieri*, its silver-grey leaves as interesting as its pine-apple-scented yellow flowers, *Cean-*

Late autumn at Oldfield.

othus 'Delight', a good, extra-hardy form, and the large, single, yellow rose, Mermaid, here thriving on a south-west wall.

Among the many prostrate junipers grown, I must pick out *J. communis* 'Hornibrookii' for special mention. It is very dwarf, and creeps along the ground, taking on the shape of whatever it covers; also a cotoneaster, *C. dammeri*, with something of the same habit. This has long trailing shoots, neat evergreen leaves, and red berries in the autumn.

The old cottages on the site dictated the layout of the garden, in as much as their gardens make a ready-made series of smaller plots, some of their old boundary walls being retained. One encloses an orchard (the trees are newly planted) with daffodils and other bulbs for a spring show. Another path at the rear of a long forgotten barn leads past a superb group of *Hebe rakaiensis*, with exquisitely arranged, neat leaves, and a rounded, dense habit of growth; also a rare weeping oak. *Quercus robur* 'Pendula', trained into an arch. *Geranium endressii*, 'Wargrave Pink', flowers all

A well placed pyracantha.

summer in the light shade of overhanging trees.

And trees are everywhere at Oldfield, pressing in on the garden, lawns and fields, and surrounding the house. In all, over a thousand have been planted since the owners moved in in 1979. A woodland walk leads past a new planting, many of which will add further autumnal tints as they mature. I noted the new birch, *Betula* 'Gold Cloud', acers, *Sorbus domestica*, the wild Service Tree, *Ulmus* 'Wredei' (a brilliant gold all summer) the beech, *Fagus sylvatica* 'Dawyck', a fastigiate form, and an elaegnus.

There is a plantation of Christmas trees, once grown for profit, but now enjoyed for their neat, conical appearance, and largely left untouched; a double avenue of Sweet Chestnut – *Castanea sativa*, used for coppicing, with subtle, yellow-brown tinged leaves, and a varied planting of oaks: Turkey, Red, Hungarian and native, interspersed with alder. The alder were still green, a good contrast with the vibrant reds and browns of the oaks, and will be removed for firewood as the choicer trees mature.

Even after ten years, banks are still being cleared for future planting. Weedkiller is used, but with care, huge sheets of black plastic covering the soil to prevent regrowth until plants are ready to go in. Another good idea is a bank devoted to climbers usually found growing vertically: *Clematis orientalis*, *Hydrangea petiolaris*, honeysuckle and vines. They are encouraged to grip the ground by a network of branches, which will rot as the plants root and mature. All this area is a mass of bluebells, primroses, crocus and self-seeded forget-me-nots in the spring.

There are beehives producing ordinary, multi-floral honey, as well as an exotic form of blackberry from the many brambles still making a dense undergrowth in the woods, and giving an inkling of what the owners faced in the garden such a short time ago. Groups of rugosa roses near the entrance, as well as many other shrubs fill the garden, but this is largely a garden of trees, beautifully in keeping with the sylvan landscape all around.

The Old Rectory, Fitz ✸ near Shrewsbury

A delightful country garden covering just over one acre and containing a wealth of interesting plants. Open under the N.G.S., see Yellow Book.

The best description I can conceive of for The Old Rectory is a sophisticated cottage garden. Sophisticated in that the gracious eighteenth century house sits in the centre of the garden giving an air of dignity to the gently sloping site; cottagey in the profusion of flowers and the artless nature of the design. There are areas of formality close to the house, but these merge seamlessly with the wilder parts of the garden.

This is very much my kind of garden. Nothing overdone, just the right amount of maintenance, and an emphasis on the plants. A perfect antidote to the overdesigned, busy, somewhat artificial gardens in favour at the moment. Covering just one acre, The Old Rectory should be a Mecca for readers with a largish country garden to lay out.

A well composed garden can come from inspired guesswork as well as a formal plan on paper, and this is the impression given at The Old Rectory. The front of the house (which was built in 1722) faces south with views of the Shropshire hills. There is a large flat lawn once dominated by a huge cedar, sadly lost in the winter of 1982 when it was completely defoliated and never recovered. This was a serious loss of a most important vertical element in the garden design.

Primula japonica thriving at The Old Rectory.

The lawn could be somewhat featureless, but the owner has tentative plans for a curved yew hedge, which would also serve to block off part of the garden, thus preventing the visitor from seeing the whole area at once. Mature trees ring this lawn: Scots Pine, yews and an interesting beech with three trunks, two green and one copper!

Two large island beds and a long border on the western side give colour and interest. Plants which caught my eye were two unusual buddleias: alternifolia, with bunches of sweet scented mauve flowers arranged along its drooping branches, and 'Harlequin', with boldly marked cream edged leaves and a dark-red terminal raceme. Also the rarely seen *Lonicera chaetocarpa*, a honeysuckle, with bell-shaped, pale cream flowers on a loose bush. It is beloved of bees.

Close by was one of the few annuals I like, *Omphaloides linifolia*: small spikes of round white flowers with grey-green foilage and a distinctive black eye. This is not lined-up in serried rows, but allowed to grow where it will, blending with the perennials.

In another bed was a fascinating, pink, double campion, *Centaurea gigantium*, with wonderful silvery 'drumsticks'; *Aquilegia* 'Nora Barlow', an unusual red and cream spurless double (there is also a black form); the yellow tree paeony lutea ludlowii and *Exochorda* 'The Bride'. The latter is a small shrub with pure white blossoms which had been in flower since February. Incredibly

The Old Rectory, Fitz.

when we saw it in May, it was still a mass of flower.

Many large, natural gardens spread in a rather aimless way and can look shapeless and weak. The Old Rectory manages to avoid this trap. There is nothing pretentious or artificial, but neither does the garden lack nucleus. This is probably because of the beautiful, mellow red-brick house and the owners' knowledge of plants, their eventual size, habit and cultural needs.

At the furthest point from the house is a woodland glade with wild flowers: hellebores, wild strawberry, foxgloves, pink purslane and primroses, many responsible for putting themselves in place. Close by is a large natural pond in an area of rough grass. No attempt has been made to over-cultivate this area, just rough wooden posts confining damp soil to make a home for candelabra primula, gunnera, and hostas. A big, single yellow rose overhangs the pool, variety unknown. It is superficially like *Rosa* 'Canary Bird', but a more subtle, paler shade, with delightful ferny leaves.

There are in fact many unusual roses in this garden, some chosen for foliage as much as flower, such as *R. farreri* 'Persetosa', the Threepenny-bit Rose, and *R. rubrifolia*. The former has minute pale-pink flowers set against small, dark green leaves, the latter, grey-mauve leaves as beautiful as any bloom and larger single pink flowers (*R. rubrifolia* will seed true).

I love this wild area, again the owner has managed not to overcook the pudding by interfering too much. The art of wild gardening is to allow vigorous plants to spread naturally without swamping each other. Easier said than done!

Perennial violas, The Old Rectory, Fitz.

Following the garden round, there is an area for vegetables in the centre of the garden between the wilder and more cultivated parts, and a wide, sheltered border backing up against an old, red brick wall. There were so many favourites here it is difficult to pick out just a few. Of special note were an elaeagnus with narrow, silver-grey leaves and a delicious scent, overgrown with the double clematis 'Vyvian Pennell'. This clematis is a tricky one to grow – it gets wilt – but is a tour de force when it thrives. Also the Snowdrop Tree, *Halesia monticola*; and a bright, white, herbaceous potentilla. The shrubby kind are well known garden favourites, but the herbaceous forms are also excellent plants and deserve to be better known.

In a raised, sheltered bed close to the house reserved for tender favourites were a well grown group of the St. Bruno Lily, *Lilastrum paradisa*. The owner was especially proud of them as she collected the seed from the Pyrenees herself.

Finally, the walls of the house provide the best background possible for an unusual double *Clematis montana*, 'Marjorie', a more subtle pink than the single forms, and the flowers last longer, also 'Mermaid', *the* single, yellow rose to grow if you have the right spot (it gets very big and doesn't like pruning). It has huge blooms, glossy green leaves, never a riot of flowers but rarely without a few all summer.

No showy ornaments in this garden, no summer houses or elaborate patios, but like a Japanese flower arrangement, its beauty depends on what the owner has had the will power to leave out.

The Old School House ❀ Upton Magna

A charming, old-world garden, surrounding a Victorian gothic cottage. Not open to the public.

It is difficult to pin down precisely what makes one warm to certain gardens. For me it is partly the setting and the house, and partly the choice of plants. That is why, when we arrived at The Old School House, I knew instinctively as we brushed past the burgeoning *Jasminum officinale* cascading over the wall close to the gate, that it was going to be my kind of garden.

The house is a typical, mid-Victorian building, constructed in 1858 of red-brick and Grinshill grey sandstone. The windows are delightful: carved in stone which might have come from a medieval church; the arched, heavily hinged front door, carrying on the Gothic theme.

Most of the garden lies to the back of the house, and is designed with perfect simplicity to make a pleasant foil for the architectural complications of the house. Briefly, there is a house at one end of the garden and a small, square orchard taking up about the same amount of space at the other. Between, the garden divides into three.

Victorian gothic charm at The Old School House.

Two vegetable sections on either side of a long grass path with parallel herbaceous and shrub borders on each side. Long wires on posts covered in climbers, cement the division between food and flower.

There are complications, such as an old laundry and the boys' and girls' lavatories, but the basic plan is plain and perfect. There was no need for curving lines or busy little paths leading nowhere, and the owner has had the strength of mind to leave both out.

The main problem with the garden when the owner moved there in 1974 was that it didn't exist! There was a tarmac playground both back and front. The solution was a J.C.B. hired by the day and seven lorry loads of somewhat clayey top soil. A load of Grinshill stone similar to that used in the house was also obtained to trim the lawn where it meets the flower border. This cuts down work edging, and gives space for flopping plants to spill over without getting in the way of the mower.

There is a cottagey feel about the planting. Profuse, simple, and in soft, old-fashioned colours. A plan was made on paper, and an attempt made to plant the smaller things in groups, but the authentic, old-world atmosphere, comes from self-seeding, and a reluctance to use the hoe. That supreme cottage garden plant, *Lychnis coronaria*, was enjoying the hot weather. The bright magenta flowers never seem to clash, perhaps because the grey-flannel leaves are such a good foil. I also noted the white form 'Alba', and the white with a cerise eye, 'Oculata'. All are wonderful in a hot, dry position, and will seed freely.

Shrubs included a good dark-red spiraea – possibly 'Bullata', the best red form, also ceanothus and lavender. Close to the house are two daphnes, *D. mezereum*, a mass of red berries in July, and *D. odora* 'Aureomarginata'. The latter was quite the biggest specimen I have ever seen, and had travelled from garden to garden with the owner. In spite of the daphne's reputation as a bad mover, this one had never flagged.

To return to the main borders: *Euphorbia wulfenii*, buddleias, *Senecio greyii*, and mallow hold the planting together; all good, even when not in flower. The background roses were just getting into their stride. Two particularly good plants noted – a white agapanthus, very tall and vigorous, with a brown edge on each flower; also the delightful *Allium spaerocephalon*, like purple drumsticks covered in bees. Clematis romping through the roses included lots of small, viticella hybrids – 'Royal Velours', a gorgeous, rich wine-red like velvet, as well as the type plant, with purple-blue flowers very profusely borne, and certainly not to be despised.

There were lots of self-sown Shirley Poppies filling odd spaces, all in those lovely, washed-out colours, some with contrasting edges. That great double poppy, 'Pink Chiffon', was also in full flower. This is a firm favourite of mine and reappears year after year in my garden with no effort from me.

The front garden at the Old School House is very small, and divided from the road by a low stone wall topped by a real, country thorn hedge (useful for keeping cows out). The entire front has simply been planted up with herbaceous perennials – no shrubs except those on the walls of the house. The perennials range from the choice to the common. Amongst the former I would include a wonderful group of *Romneya coulteri*, the Californian Poppy. The owner bought three, knowing their reputation as hard to establish; inevitably all took, making an impressive group. Next to them was *Anthemis tinctoria* in the cool lemon-yellow form 'E.C. Buxton', in my opinion infinitely superior to the gaudy, bright yellow, type plant.

Yellow, white and blue are the dominant colour scheme in the front, with *Clematis orientalis* on the house, great clumps of white daisies, *Chrysanthemum maximum*, *Senecio greyii*, mauvy-blue creeping thyme and an unusual wisteria, a dark, double called 'Black Dragon'.

This was quite one of the most enjoyable gardens we visited.

The Old Vicarage ❀ Cardington

A two and a half acre country garden with wonderful views, and a rare, timeless atmosphere. Open under the N.G.S., see Yellow Book.

The owner describes this garden as scenic, which my dictionary defines as picturesque. That it certainly is. My overwhelming impression, however, is of a garden with a definite masculine air, an understated restraint which I find very attractive in this age of over-designed, over-full gardens.

The whole area is dominated by the beautiful, early nineteenth century house, built in the local grey-fawn sandstone. The owner is fortunate the house is so fine, as it sits confidently on the top of a slope and is visible from every part of the garden. The house and grounds were purchased from the Church Commissioners in 1969, the garden being described by the owner as a jungle, though there were the remnants at the side of a formal Victorian garden.

One enormous asset however were the quite magnificent trees. Huge beeches with smooth, grey-green trunks, contrasting with an equally large, rough-barked, sweet chestnut, obviously all of considerable age. Rooks cawed hoarsely in the branches all

The water garden at The Old Vicarage.

the time we were in the garden, adding greatly to the atmosphere.

Starting at the bottom of the slope and working upwards towards the house, one first comes upon two natural ponds and a narrow stream. The former providing a home for a vibrant display of candelabra primula. The incandescent, vermilion-orange would be almost too much, were it not toned down by the surrounding soft green of pond, hedges, grass, ferns and trees. Other good primula here are *P. bulleyana*, the creamy yellow sikkimensis, and secundiflora. *P. ioessa*, which I do not know, is a wonderful dusty pink, very distinctive.

Mown paths in this part of the garden, are bordered by the wild flowers: bluebells and campions. Hostas have a border to themselves against a background hedge. Shrub roses, mostly rugosas which will flourish in unfavourable conditions, are planted in island beds close to the pools.

Further up the slope, the beds are filled with conifers. These are chosen with great care to give a contrast in shape, colour and texture of foliage. The delightful, blue-tinged *Chamaecyparis pisifera* 'Boulevard' looked especially good. Mine is a martyr to red spider mite. The conifer beds are mulched with gravel over plastic sheeting to keep the weeds out and moisture in. Much appreciated by the plants if one can judge from their condition. Three hebes in the bed, cupressoides, rakaiensis and 'Pagei', fooled me at first, they are so much like conifers from a distance.

At this point, one comes unexpectedly upon a miniature fort and a full sized cannon. Strangely, they do not look in the least out of place, but appear quite at home in an English country garden. The cannon can actually (and often is) fired. The fort came from the owners' previous home in Cheshire, where it was originally built on a small island. It has lost its roof of lead and timber, but is beautifully weathered to a similar colour as the beech trunks. Perhaps that is why it fits in so well.

As we are now half way up the hill towards the house, I must mention the raised bed mulched with gravel: a mass of saxifraga, single alpine pinks, flat thymes, sisyrinchium, hardy geranium and lewisia, the latter clinging to the stones around the side. Nothing very rare or difficult, but a notable success. Just the right amount of structural firmness being added by low dwarf conifers.

A shrub border close to the house, contains weigelas, potentilla, viburnums and rhododendron. Martagon lilies slip between the shrubs. This excellent, Turk's cap lily, in soft mauvey-pink or white, is a native plant and will naturalise well in grass and light shade. It never looks better than when used in a semi-naturalised shrub border like the one at The Old Vicarage, and, unlike some lilies, is quite trouble free.

There is a bed of azaleas near the house, and another of roses close by for later colour. These are mainly the floribunda, 'Arthur Bell', a strong yellow, and, 'Glenfiddich', described by the owner, as orange-yellow. He recommends them both, as being pest resistant and very strong growing.

I liked the ramblers strung on wire providing a background, and the low growing roses, 'The Fairy', 'Snow Carpet', and 'Nozomi', for the foreground.

The house itself, plays host to a number of climbers, including a 'Virginia Creeper', *Parthenocissus quinquefolia*, which must be quite spectacular in the autumn. But I was especially interested in a wisteria, which, although it never flowers profusely, has the most intriguing, *double* flowers in mauve.

There are several reasons why wisteria does not flower well. Age, bird damage to the buds, incorrect pruning, or just not having a floriferous specimen, being the main ones. Make sure you get a grafted, not a seed raised one to avoid the last problem.

The front of the house (which was once the rear) opens into a small courtyard, which is beautifully sheltered. The owner states that everything planted there flourishes exceedingly well, as it enjoys a natural mulch from the leaves on the surrounding trees. I think the same could be said for the whole garden.

The Paddocks ❀ Chelmarsh Common

An interesting, medium sized garden, in the process of renovation. Open under the N.G.S., see Yellow Book.

The Paddocks is directly next door to a garden described earlier in the book – Dingle Bank. The owners made a gate in the hedge after hailing one another over the top, and now enjoy much swopping of cuttings and plant buying expeditions. They also open conjointly, under the National Garden Scheme.

The gardens are very different in style however. The owners of The Paddocks have only lived there for about five years, and although they have accomplished much, the garden has yet to mature and display its full potential.

The front, which is of good size, is a typical cottage mixture of annuals, perennials and climbers, most of the latter grown over a wooden pergola which extends the full length of the central path. There was nothing in the front garden but apple trees when the owners moved in, but their twisted, leaning trunks help to give the new garden character. The four-hundred year old brick and stone house also adds to the sense of continuity. It was once a row of coal miners cottages and the well which served the entire block is preserved outside the front door.

All paths and terracing are built from the materials salvaged from the renovation. One interesting idea, is a dining room with hedge walls, a barbecue, white cast iron garden furniture and a seat set into the bank, the latter ablaze with primroses early in the year.

Another enclosed area is paved and planted up with miniature roses: 'Golden Globe' yellow, 'Scarletta' a good red, 'Anna Ford' orangey, and 'Sweet Dreams' a lovely peachy colour. Box hedging is used as a border, and *Buddleia alternifolia* for a centre piece.

On the other side of the central pergola, a terracotta, Royal Doulton pixie, dating from about 1910, sits cross-legged, looking into a round pond. A delightfully original garden ornament, like nothing I have ever seen before. He is backed by a raised bed, where the centre piece is a golden leaved gleditsia.

A wide herbaceous border to the left of the drive was bright with a good selection of summer flowers – *Crocosmia* 'Lucifer', in wonderful firey red, *Potentilla* 'Elizabeth', an

The Paddocks is graced by a Royal Doulton pixie.

old favourite, but still holding its own, lychnis, dark-red berberis, and that excellent, variegated, Pineapple Mint.

At the rear of the house, a steep bank leads down to the same stream that flows through The Dingle's garden. The bank is part natural, and part constructed from the tons of rubble left over from the house renovations. It proved a convenient way to hide it without too much effort.

New apple trees have been planted here – Coxes, Jupiter, and a Bramley to carry on when the old trees die. The stream has been dammed to produce more water. Voles, toads and frogs appreciate this; while deer from the nearby Wyre Forest look over the fence, but thankfully cannot enter.

The river doesn't flood, and can be planted right up to the edge with a variety of damp loving perennials. There is a lovely view up the slope towards the house, looking over a good stand of *Macleaya cordata*, the Plume Poppy. This is a very tall perennial, grown as much for its foliage – large, lobed, grey-green leaves – as the creamy flowers. It stands up well in spite of its height, and though it does run a little, never in an invasive way.

This garden still has some way to go, everything cannot be done at once (in fact I am a strong advocate of living with a garden for a while before making any irrevocable decisions) but the owners have certainly made a promising start.

Parsons Pleasure ❀ Acton Burnell

A largish, young garden, on an open site, containing some of the best herbaceous perennials in the county. Not open to the public.

The owner of Parsons Pleasure is a plantswoman right down to the ends of her green fingers. She has lived in the house for only five years, and, although the garden is not unnaturally somewhat flat (there were no large trees), parts already have a mature, lived in, feel. The owner has had an interest in both unusual and superior forms of herbaceous perennials for many years. The garden abounds with them, as well as numerous variegated plants, for which she also has a long standing passion.

From the road outside, it is obvious that this is an enthusiast's garden. Everything is the best of its kind. Even the common valerian in the stone wall at the front of the house grows thicker and redder than any other I have seen.

Although the garden is young, the house it surrounds is old. The black and white medieval half was once part of the parson's glebe; though it also figures in ancient records as both a bawdy house and an inn! The garden surrounds the house, but the greater part is at the rear, where the gently undulating lawn is divided into several very large beds. The front of the house is slightly raised above the road, the soil held back by a low, dry-stone wall, which plays host to a number of sun-loving plants.

One is a group of the large *Sempervivum* 'Othello': a lovely dark red colour, and quite the best form to look out for. Also close to this wall – or actually in it – was a well-grown example of *Euphorbia characias*, with spikes of green flowers and dark brown centres, a very dark leaved sedum and the common Curry Plant, *Helichrysum italicum*, its narrow, grey leaves contrasting with the green and obviously thriving in the well-drained, sandy soil. Nearby are self-sown poppies, a semi-double orange superficially like the double form of *Meconopsis cambrica* 'Flore Pleno'. Self-sown campanulas also fight for a place with the other plants, in every cool tint from white through all shades of blue. In fact, the whole garden is a mixture of the sophisticated and the cottagey. New perennials only read about or glimpsed at Chelsea, jostling with old-fashioned favourites.

At the rear it's hard to pick out plants for special mention, there are so many noteable forms. Ones that stood out for me were an interesting example of the Potato Vine, *Solanum crispum*, its foliage beautifully variegated in dark green and cream. It looked wonderful, smothered in small, dark mauve flowers, and was grown prostrate as a mound, not trained as a climber. I also adore all the eryngiums, especially alpinum with its delicate ruff in steely-blue. Here I saw an extra fine form with a double lace collar – absolutely outstanding.

The owner of Parsons Pleasure is an iris specialist.

At the top of a dry wall grows a creamy pink achillea. There are now many shades of these ferny-leaved, flat-headed flowers (close relations of the common Yarrow). I like the ordinary yellow kinds, both the tall *A. filipendulina* 'Gold Plate', and the shorter 'Moonshine', and have grown 'Cerise Queen' in a lovely magenta-pink for many years, but the new Galaxy Hybrids have opened up a whole new world of colours, from rich-red to sugar-pink.

This garden holds the National Collection of epimediums. These delightful plants, excellent ground cover, but also beautiful if not spectaclar in flower, are grown chiefly for their pretty leaves. They like a cool, shady position, and the leaves colour well in the autumn. I find the small flowers on wiry stems, as well as the leaves, cut well and last a long time in a vase. The owner is also an iris specialist. There were many examples in flower, some completely unknown to me, but I especially admired a beautiful group of *Iris kaempferi*, with

Eryngium alpinium *in a superb double ruffed form.*

flat flowers on long stems, looking surprisingly happy in an ordinary bed. I always assumed they had to have wet soil on a pond margin to thrive.

Tall plants for the back of the border grown at Parsons Pleasure include a pale pink Tree Mallow, or lavatera; a very subtle colour compared to the common, rather hard, vibrant pink usually seen, but otherwise identical in habit of growth; also a dark mauve mallow which I grow myself, which was quite as large as the Tree Mallow (I suspect it is not hardy). Foxtail Lilies, or eremurus, waved gracefully in the breeze high above the other perennials. These magnificent flowers have long, straight stems set with many tiny flowers at the top, and no leaves to speak of. They come in many colours, white, pink and cream, and are somewhat tricky to grow, as their star-shaped roots are easily damaged and resent disturbance. They also get frosted in cold winters, as you cannot plant them too deep. The best advice I can give is to choose an easy form, I have had most success with *E. stenophyllus*, a lovely clear yellow, and cover with a mound of peat over winter.

One cannot but wonder at the variety of plants in this garden, a treasure house chosen with a true gardener's eye.

Pitchford Hall ❀ Pitchford

An important Elizabethan manor house, sited in a hollow. Open under the N.G.S., see Yellow Book.

The garden at Pitchford Hall is an intriguing mix of the formal and informal. The informal comprises banks of daffodils and primroses, together with a large lake surrounded by mature trees. The formal incorporates several sheltered courtyards each with a character all its own. One, close to the rear of the house, brooded over by a quartet of peacocks looming like vultures on the high walls; another, stiff with clipped yews.

Pitchford Hall itself is described as the most splendid piece of black and white building in Shropshire and it dominates the garden. Built by a Shrewsbury woollen merchant in 1560 – 70, the first thing that strikes one is its enormous size. Then, the fact that it sits comfortably in a depression, so that one must look up at the garden from most rooms in the house. Only over the river is there a view of surrounding hills and fields.

Perhaps this is why the famous black and white tree house, constructed in the 1760's, was built into the branches of a European Lime. From its windows the vista reaches as far as the Wrekin. A superb avenue of Common Lime, *Tilia × europaea*, stretches from one of the lodges to the house, and another group of limes, covered in mistletoe, face the front of the house across a flat and formal lawn now used for croquet.

I loved the half buried gazebo in a corner of this lawn: one quarter slice of a round cake, its roof a mass of lichen and polypodium ferns. The enclosed kitchen garden has a magnificent wall covered in espalier apples and pears, while the walls opposite the front of the house play host to forsythia, *Prunus laurocerasus* 'Otto Luyken', roses and honeysuckle.

The house was neglected up to the end of the 1950's, when it was acquired by a member of the original family who owned the property, and restoration begun. Mr. Tolley, the gardener, has looked after the grounds for over twenty-six years, their restoration running parallel with that of the house.

One can only surmise what the original gardens were like when the house was built. Their contents can be identified from such books as 'Gerard's Herball', published in 1597, or his catalogue of plants growing in his own garden at Holborn. A large house such as Pitchford probably contained a fair percentage of the plants mentioned in these two books. The reign of Elizabeth saw the first great wave of plant introductions to this country. Hybridization was also producing a host of new varieties, more especially among carnations, tulips, iris, lily and lilacs to name but a few. All these

A wing of Pitchford Hall.

new plants added greatly to the garden scene at the time Pitchford was being built and in the years shortly afterwards, when the original gardens were being laid out.

Some other important features might have been a knot garden, probably on the flat site, close to the house, now the croquet lawn. There was great emphasis on perfume as well as colour: low clipped hedges of box, lavender, or other herbs. Fruit trees, topiary, and sheltered, close walks overhung with roses or pleached limes also played a part. The Elizabethans enjoyed ornaments: stone fountains and sundials marking focal points. One must not forget too the part played by bees, many gardens containing bee hives or straw skeps to supply the house in those far off, sugar-free times.

There are no rare and exotic plants at Pitchford, but the situation, atmosphere and sheer presence of the great house make it an unforgettable gardening experience.

Preen Manor ✹ Church Preen

A large garden covering some six acres, consisting of a series of interconnected smaller gardens, set in the ruins of a Cluniac monastery. Open under the N.G.S., see Yellow Book.

Walking around Preen Manor is an enlightening experience, because one realises at once that this is a garden with literally everything.

First the situation – it is set amidst beautiful rolling hills with fine views over totally unspoilt countryside. Then the house – built in the seventeenth century of mellow sandstone taken from the previous buildings on the site, a twelfth century Cluniac abbey, parts of which are incorporated into the garden design. Add the magnificent trees – mature cedars dating from Victorian times, and the oldest yew in the county, reputedly planted in AD 457. Include the aspect – seven hundred feet above sea level, but protected from cold winds by thick woodland. Best of all, Preen Manor garden has the advantage of owners who are obviously devoted to its further improvement and upkeep.

It would be difficult to digest the garden in one short visit if it were not, wisely, broken up into more manageable slices. For it is a garden of gardens, each with a separate character and distinctive identity all its own. The whole design of the garden was achieved by trial and error, nothing was written down on paper. Looking at the result, I can certainly recommend living with a garden as an excellent way to find out what will and will not work.

The bones of the garden in the shape of mature trees, well-built walls, and well-defined changes of level, were of course already in place. This is an old garden in the sense that the land has been occupied for many generations, the present owners having utilized all the architectural elements they inherited to the best advantage. Cleverly, they have modelled new work on the old. This is especially evident in the vegetable garden, whose elaborate, double-arrow ground plan, echoes the high brick and stone wall bordering one side. Even the metal arches used to support roses and beans mirror this shape. In one tiny garden built round a shallow, stone-filled pool, and entirely enclosed, a cut-out wooden fence acts as a foil for *Lonicera giraldii*, an evergreen species of honeysuckle with heart-shaped leaves and purplish-red flowers and also *Parthenocissus henryana*, a superb self-clinging vine with good autumn colour, and *Clematis* 'Henryi', with huge white flowers. All these will soften the hard edges as they grow.

A palette of greens at Preen Manor.

But, to begin at the beginning: one realises this garden is something special as you approach the house. The upper storey and roof seem to float above a mauve sea of Rhododendron ponticum. There are touches of other, choicer colours, but the overall impression is of undulating acres of purple. Next, the road winds between mysterious trees with twisted trunks, which, in turn, give way to a wide open space in front of the house where an entrance gate and short expanse of wall are all that remain of the Norman Shaw mansion that once occupied the site. The magnificent cedars which fronted it are still standing however, and provide a dramatic feature across the terraced lawn. They break the flatness of this formally designed area with their great bulk, the horizontal growth of the dark-green foliage echoing the grass terracing.

The present house is built around three sides of a courtyard, but the front encompasses a sloping lawn and the paved Vestry Garden. A list of the plants in this small garden alone would fill the entire chapter, sufficient to say that the owners have the knowledge to use a very wide repertoire of plants, some unusual and all beautiful. They have that rare knack of planting for detail without ever losing sight of the whole. One or two plants however, must be mentioned: first, a well-grown mulberry. I know little about this tree, other than it is difficult to establish. I believe the brittle roots call for especial care in planting. The specimen at Preen Manor looks wonderful, and, as the species was introduced in the sixteenth century, is certainly in keeping with the historical atmosphere.

In the Cottage Garden nearby is *Prunus serrula*, with perhaps the most beautiful bark of any small tree. This one is perfectly placed so that one can indulge in the irresistible urge to stroke its smooth, red, polished trunk. The owner carefully prunes the upper branches so that its full beauty is revealed.

To the side of the front lawn, great clumps of an unusual, delicate pink Oriental Poppy lean towards the grass. Nor are the common forgotten: I noted purple sage, valerian (*the* plant for walls) the trailing hardy geranium, 'Buxton's Blue', helianthemum and aquilegia. The deep-green, ferny passageway leading to the Secret Garden next door, is a lovely contrast to the tailored lawns and profusion of bright flowers. I repeat, it would be easier to make a list of what is *not* in the garden.

The Chess Garden is an interesting concept. The owners were faced with a swimming pool garden which they did not wish to retain, and, have planted an enclosed lawn with a sunken area, laid out with a chess board pattern and giant sized chess pieces. The owner states that she wishes she had used yew hedges instead of beech, but I rather liked the contrasting purple and green, even if the leaves do make a mess when they drop.

My favourite part of the garden is the damp area to the right of the house. This contains two long pools, one above the other, which date from 1150, and are known as the Monk's Bathing Pools. They are fed by a natural stream running under a delightful stone bridge, and each can be emptied and cleaned with the aid of giant plugs. The shady area close to the bridge is home to a variety of plants which enjoy the wet conditions: Primula japonica in variety, rodgersias with their huge, architectural leaves, and hostas, as well as selfsown foxgloves and ferns. The whole area is dominated by a wonderful yew, its ancient trunk, a tangled conglomeration of smaller branches and roots hard to describe, but quite unforgettable to anyone who appreciates abstract, sculptural forms.

The great banks of rhododendron are threaded with a walk which one can reach from this point. Close too, the choicer specimens can be picked out and admired. A tall wall at the top of the rhododendron bank shelters large shrubs which like some protection from cold winds, such as *Buddleia globosa* from Chile. This is a very striking shrub,

Dramatic sculpted yews, the Monks' Bathing Pools.

nothing like an ordinary buddleia, with tiny, orange, golf-ball flowers.

A complete contrast again, is the totally enclosed courtyard at the rear of the house. The walls here are utilized for really fragile beauties. Of particular interest at the time we visited was *Lonicera × tellmanniana*, with extra large, bright, orange-copper flowers. I have seen it stated this plant does best in shade, but at Preen it flourishes in full sun. *L.ciliosa*, 'Dropmore Scarlet', is another different honeysuckle here, with scarlet, tubular flowers, which grows exceptionally well.

It is, of course, hard to go wrong in this garden with such a wonderful skeleton to clothe, but the owners have certainly made the most of it: creating in only eleven years one of the best private gardens in Shropshire.

Ridgeway Wood ❀ near Craven Arms

A twenty acre woodland garden open under the N.G.S., see Yellow Book.

Ridgeway Wood is appropriately named as it does in fact consist almost entirely of coniferous woodland. Apart from a sloping lawn on the south side of the house laid out with island beds, the whole area is a series of woodland walks mown through the thick forest.

Mysterious dark treescapes crowd in on all sides. The sunlight is filtered through the feathery overhead shade of a million tiny needles, and one is conscious only of bird song and the far away bleat of sheep. A perfect place to stop, rest and contemplate nature.

Rhododendrons, azaleas and heather beds flourish near the wood-framed, cedar-shingled, low-pitched house – perfectly in tune with its woodland setting – but for me the main delight of this garden is its wild flowers: pink campion, blue bells of course, violets – mauve and white – Enchanter's Nightshade, Shuttlecock Ferns, wild strawberries, Herb Robert, Ladies Bedstraw and Stitchwort all in one, small, damp, shady area. Earlier come the primroses: later dog roses and exotic wild orchids, their spotted leaves already piercing the green moss lining the path. Closer to the house in a more open position grow toadflax and a tiny yellow creeping plant so like our garden ajuga or Bugle, they must be related.

In the wilder, woodland areas, no attempt has been made to clear brambles or bracken, but all seem to exist harmoniously; the heavy shade deeper in amongst the trees, pushing out the more noxious weeds. Parts of the wood are being replanted: I noted a delightful copse of young Scots Pine.

Woodland paths at Ridgeway Wood.

Trees in a garden always attract birds, and this garden must be perfect for observation. Efforts have been made by the owners to encourage birds by providing nesting boxes, but with such natural advantages it hardly seems necessary. Not only is the garden set in beautiful, unspoilt countryside, but deciduous woods are also plentiful in the near vicinity, thus ensuring sightings of all the birds who enjoy these varied conditions.

As so many of our wild flowers are facing a threat from intensive farming, urbanisation and the use of pesticides, it is well worth anyone who has the space – a small paddock, a tiny patch of woodland, a boggy area too damp to plant properly – considering giving the area over to wild flowers. It is important, however, to choose the plants which fit, or go along with the natural conditions in your garden. Ridgeway Wood is filled with wild flowers which enjoy shade, or the dappled light of a clearing. By studying the wild flora of the part of the county in which you live, the soil conditions, micro-climate, etc., you can save yourself many disappointments. It is usually better to grow on the seed (which is readily obtainable from seedsmen now) into small plants, rather than scatter indiscriminately, though some green-fingered people *can* get away with the latter method. For the majority, however, plug planting into grass sward will give the greatest measure of success. Remember to look out for what grows locally and follow. Never feed with any fertilizer once planted, or you will encourage the grass at the expense of the flowers.

There is a hidden vegetable garden close to the house, discreetly sheltered by a tall beech hedge. A choisya in full flower fills the air with perfume, but even here the wild theme, with rampant species clematis, honeysuckle and wild Welsh poppies seems to dominate the scene.

A bizarre final touch: in a neighbouring field a camel leisurely cropped the grass in company with goats and horses, eyeing us with stony dignity as we goggled and exclaimed. A refugee from a summer travelling circus, he appeared as perfectly at home as the rooks above our heads.

Ruthall Manor ❁ Ditton Priors

A one acre garden packed with interesting plants, including a natural water garden. Open under the N.G.S., see Yellow Book.

Ruthall Manor was first mentioned in the Domesday Book. It now consists of a square, Georgian house and farm buildings, with a well laid out garden on the south-west side of the property. This is hardly surprising, as the present owner is a professional landscape gardener.

Her interest began in her own garden, which she completely reorganized after the disastrous winter of 1982 (though the mature trees are earlier). The interest blossomed, then developed into an invitation to design friends' gardens. Now, after an intensive course at the Inchbold Garden Design School, she constructs both public and private gardens, including that round the castle at Bridgnorth, as well as several parks in the same town.

I enjoyed all parts of Ruthall Manor garden, but the most memorable for me, was the superbly planted pool. Originally constructed as a horse pond, where the animals could drink at the end of a day's work, it is paved on the farm side with large stones to prevent the giant hooves digging up the mud. Across the pond is a steep bank with natural shade. There is a marshy area on the left – always a wonderful asset.

The surroundings were a blaze of colour from the candelabra primulas when we visited it in mid-June. There are named varieties – 'Inverewe', 'Postford White', 'Miller's Crimson', but for me, the hybrids in all shades of pink, cream orange and red were equally beautiful. Each block of colour merged into the next, yellow blending to subtle buttery creams, orange and red, in a veritable rainbow. Tonal changes and depth of colour are regulated by the dappled shade from an overgrown thorn hedge. So often one sees one or two plants, painstakingly placed; how marvellous to have room to let them spread naturally. *Mimulus* 'Whitecroft Scarlet', faded to a vibrant orange in the hot sun, was also a picture, as were the blue *Iris Kaempferi*, twice as big as I have ever seen before in the deep, fertile mud.

The rest of the garden consists of beds for tender plants close to the house, a large, oval lawn to the front, a woodland area to one side, and a vegetable garden on the other.

I must mention the interesting wrought iron work which separates the border from the vegetables. This was especially commissioned by the owner, and made by Mr. Rob Thorne at the Maws Centre, Coalbrookdale. It fits snugly into the garden, and, as well as acting as a divider, provides excellent support for a number of plants, including a superb, dark blue-purple *Clematis* × *durandii*.

The old horsepond at Ruthall Manor.

There is a good windbreak of conifers around the woodland area, enabling several very unusual trees to flourish. Notable were a variegated Tulip Tree, *Liriodendron tulipifera* 'Aureomarginatum', *Eucalyptus pauciflora*, The Snow Gum, with snow-white trunk; and *Acer cappadocicum*. The latter is especially rare in the variety grown; 'Aureum'. The young leaves are red, turning to a golden-yellow as they mature. A delightful medium sized tree, perfectly hardy in this country, *if* you can get hold of it.

I also admired *Tropaeolum speciosum*, the climbing, flame-coloured perennial, draping itself over *Cedrus deodara*; a lovely way to grow this difficult plant. It must be started from a pot grown specimen, as the roots resent disturbance, and it likes damp, light shade. Don't give in easily; I succeeded on the third try. It is one of those plants which, once established, romps away.

An unusual clematis, superficially rather like montana, is also grown on a tall conifer, namely *C. chrysocoma var. sericea*. I must admit, the dark, evergreen needles prove a wonderful background for vigorous clematis. Three tips – choose tough varieties, any of the montanas are ideal, don't plant too close, and water until established. Lastly, plant on the side of the tree where the prevailing wind will blow the clematis *into* the tree, not away from the branches. All this woodland area at Ruthall is underplanted with bulbs: hardy cyclamen and *Anemone blanda*.

The last tree I must mention – though there are many more equally fine is *Paulownia fargesii*. This is a superb flowering tree (though it rarely does so in this climate) with the most enormous furry leaves. It must have sun and shelter, and doesn't like a shallow soil, but if you *can* grow one, do. Fargesii is a better form than the usual tomentosa, as it is hardier, and flowers earlier. The trick is to get the flower buds through the winter, when they come out fully in May. Easier said than done!

Other tender shrubs which flourish include *Cytisus battandieri*, not often seen flowering so well away from a warm wall, its pineapple scent filling the air, and *Carpentaria california*. The latter does have some protection from the house, but again I was amazed to see it doing so well away from a wall, the whole large shrub a mass of white flowers with bright, golden centres.

So many unusual plants are grown, it is difficult not to sound like a list. Each one carefully sited to exploit its natural habit of growth: helianthemums spreading over paving stones, plants which bloom early and then disappear, backed by others which come into their own later. A true plantswoman's garden, but also a lovely garden to learn in the best possible way – by example – how to place perennials, trees and shrubs to the best advantage.

Helianthemum and Dianthus over the path.

Stanley Hall ❀ Bridgnorth

A rhododendron and azalea garden with architecturally distinguished Jacobean house. Open under the N.G.S., see Yellow Book.

The glories of Stanley Hall are the great banks of rhododendron which line the long drive to the house, and the huge trees in the park, both native and exotic. The wide lawns around the orange brick and red sandstone Jacobean house are dotted with some of the most magnificent specimens of conifers and deciduous trees. More especially, the largest copper beeches I have ever seen, as well as great mounds of golden, Irish Yew – *Taxus baccata* 'Fastigiata' – rising like yellow flames above the dark green rhododendron. The twisted, indented trunks of the Sweet Chestnut, contrast with the giant, jigsaw-like pieces on the sides of the Scots Pine – our only native pine incidentally. The variety of bark alone is amazing, while the shapes and colours of the foliage, smooth, green ovals, against feathery pine needles, are breathtaking.

Huge trees at Stanley Hall.

Only time can produce trees of this venerable size and maturity, and time Stanley Hall (the name means stone hall) certainly has had. There is evidence that the fish ponds were constructed by monks from the Priory at Morville, but the present house took shape in 1642, though it is believed the original plans were never completed. It then passed through several hands, until, in about 1808 – 15, it was extended by Sir Thomas Tyrwhitt. The house was almost demolished in 1923, but saved in the nick of time by a forebear of the present owner, though the house had already been partially destroyed. The main tree planting was undertaken soon after Sir Thomas Tyrwhitt's renovations in the early nineteenth century, it is thought, with the assistance of Planter Wood of Dudmaston.

The rhododendrons were laid out from 1880 onwards, when these wonderfully exotic plants were first discovered in great numbers, and their potential in massed, woodland planting, realised. They must have made a tremendous impression on the Victorians, who were delighted to use them in vast numbers in their parks and gardens, where these foreign beauties signalled their liking for the damp British climate. Stanley Hall garden is of course a largely nineteenth century concept. A design contemporary with the house would have included patterned knot gardens, mazes, formal pools and canals.

The outbuildings, stable block, cottages and Garden House, are as interesting as the hall itself. Most have been adapted to provide homes for various members of the family. The small office, built of the same mellow orange brick as the main house, has a delightful, self-contained garden, of lychnis, Lambs Ears, Day Lilies, Hollyhocks, potentillas and santolina. The glorious blue hydrangea in a corner, pointing out the extreme acidity of the light, sandy loam.

A sunken, paved, courtyard garden lies on two sides of the main house. There are large, wide urns, planted with brilliant geraniums to mark the steps, while raised borders are full of lavender, honeysuckle and valerian. Shrubs include the floribunda rose 'Iceberg', and prostrate *Cotoneaster horizontalis*.

Well away from the main house, behind an ancient box hedge, is a deep hollow with a long, green pond, its sides hung with native trees, creating a paradise for wildlife. Rabbits scuttle, pigeons clap the air with their wings, pheasants clatter in the far away woods, insects hum. Tiny open sided summer houses are dotted strategically about the garden, so that one can sit and enjoy the tranquil atmosphere.

The view from the front of the house across the wide lawn is terminated by a balustrade which came from The Garth, near Welshpool. This was a large, important house, designed by Loudon in 1808, now sadly demolished. The unusual pierced stonework, wrought-iron gate and shell motifs, once separated the main lawn from the village cricket pitch! There is now a corn field where the crack of wood on willow once rang out.

The long drive to the house is, of course, chiefly renowned for the rhododendrons and azaleas, but in early spring, bluebells carpet the thin grass

A balustrade divides the garden from fields.

under the trees. The avenue of chestnuts replaced the original planting of limes – this *is* a seventeenth century idea, the double row of trees in parallel being remarked on in surviving records of gardens from this period.

An old oak close to the house is completely hollow, making an authentic tree house for successive generations of the family. The whole atmosphere is that of a lived in and loved private garden, in spite of the size of the house. Good as the National Trust are, they cannot help slightly institutionalising properties they take over. It is sadly inevitable, making gardens like that at Stanley Hall, still in private hands, a real treasure.

A final note: Pickwick was filmed at Stanley Hall a year or so ago, the house and grounds being considered a very passable imitation of the famed Dingley Dell.

Swallow Hayes ❀ Albrighton

A large, modern garden, packed with interesting plants emphasising all year round interest and ease of maintenance. Open under the N.G.S., see Yellow Book.

Unlike the vast majority of gardens included in this book, Swallow Hayes is a comparatively new garden surrounding a modern house designed by the owners. Their livelihood was an expanding nursery dealing in roses, shrubs and perennials, so the two acres were planned to be trial grounds and a source of cuttings for the nursery, as well as providing an appropriate setting for the house and giving pleasure to its occupants.

In such a large, well stocked garden, ease of maintenance had to be an important consideration, and the owner estimates that it requires an average of only eight hours upkeep per week to maintain it at what I would consider is little short of perfection. An incredible feat as no gardener is employed.

Swallow Hayes contains a tunnel of **Prunus yoshino 'Pendula'.**

The ground, which is well drained sandy loam, slopes gently away from the house towards fields full of nursery stock and the Shropshire plain. The Clee Hills and the Wrekin are far away on the distant horizon.

There are no corners visible within the basic oblong shape, the garden design being based on island beds with sinuous, wide, green paths between. As befits the owner of a nursery, the lawn is superbly maintained.

The whole point of Swallow Hayes are the hardy trees, shrubs and perennials, and there is a wonderful selection of choice plants on display. It is simply impossible to mention anything other than a very small number which took my eye at the season we visited – mid May. A visit at another time of the year would produce a totally different list. The owner has an incredible 1,500 plants named.

Starting at the front of the house, I noticed two large double gorse bushes each side of the entrance. Huge mounds of bright yellow, smelling distinctly of desiccated coconut, *Ulex europaeus plena* is a much underrated plant. I love it. The owner tells me she has a sport which is even more full – a double, double? It is being propagated for sale later. In the rest of the garden, conifers which I particularly admired were *Chamaecyparis obtusa* 'Crippsii', a small, slow growing tree, with rich, chrome-yellow foliage and an elegant habit of growth; also *Pinus wallichiana*, the Bhutan Pine. It has long, blue-green needles on drooping branches, a very graceful and attractive species. I grow *Picea pungens* 'Koster', in my own garden. It is lovely in the spring, each blue branch sporting a duck-egg blue shaving brush of new growth at the end. There is a small but well grown specimen of *Picea brewerana*, Brewer's Weeping Spruce, one of the most beautiful of all the ornamental conifers, with long green curtains of foliage hanging from each drooping branch. This conifer is so much in demand it is not easy to obtain, and is equally difficult to place and grow successfully. We saw it just before the long fronds of new growth made it an even more impressive sight.

I must mention the extremely rare *Colletia armata* which comes from South America and looks as if it ought to be very tender, but survived 26 degrees of frost in the 1982 winter, and must therefore be considered one hundred per cent sound. It is a strange plant, about eight feet high, its branches and leaves consisting of tough, rounded spines. The owner tells me the flowers smell of custard! There is a pink form, 'Rosea', which is rather more difficult to obtain.

Ceanothus 'Delight' in full flower at Swallow Hayes.

Among the deciduous trees was a large specimen of *Acer davidii* with striped green and white bark, earning it the common name of Snake Bark Maple. The owner has seen the plant in the wild, but assured me that the tree at Swallow Hayes exceeded even them in girth. At the bottom of the garden are a group of birches with wonderful bright, white bark. They are superficially similar to *Betula jacquemontii*, but are thought by Roy Lancaster, who is familiar with the garden, to be hybrids with *B.utilis*. He has observed them in the Himalayas, where their territories overlap. Another good birch for the small garden quite new to me was *B.nigra*, the River Birch, with brownish, shaggy bark, not unlike *Acer griseum*. A fine tree for damp ground, this one is from the United States.

Not only rare and difficult plants have a place in this garden, the sweet scented *Gallium odorata*, Woodruff, a native wild flower and self-sown Honesty, softening the edges of the shrub borders with a purple haze, add a natural touch.

To the right of the house is the winter garden where the owner grows the National Collection of Hamamelis, or Witch Hazel, underplanted with heather. I am not fond of heather en masse, but these are broken up with other shrubs to give height and interest.

The garden's pièce de résistance is a weeping cherry, *Prunus yoshino* 'Pendula', which covers a flight of stone steps and boast a path through its drooping branches. A wonderful sight at any time, but spectacular when in flower.

Talbot Street ❀ Ellesmere

A small, walled town garden, at the rear of a black and white, timber-framed house. Not open to the public.

This is a town garden in every sense of the word – small, compact, surrounded by walls and other houses; but also – windless, manageable, and delightfully private. The owners found an overgrown mass of brambles and raspberries when they moved in twelve years ago. It had in fact been virtually ignored for fifteen years by the previous owner. Digging revealed treasure in the form of bricks and stone, which – with other old materials bought in – made a sound basis for the garden plan. The ground slopes up from the house, so steps and a terrace were constructed. The square garden above is designed round a circular lawn with island beds.

The owner states that she has no colour plan, but simply walks around the garden with a plant in one hand and a trowel in the other, looking for a space. I guess this system works for her, because she tends to choose soft colours and interesting foliage, shying away instinctively from the garish. She finds it hard to visualise colour schemes in her head, but has great admiration for those who do. I found the mixture of old-fashioned, cottage garden flowers – pinks, artemisia, lavender, rue, rosemary, and other herbs grown for visual effect, quite charming.

Variegated plants are a particular feature. Some really unusual ones noted were a variegated artemisia, and variegated nasturtium. The former has lovely foliage anyway, usually in a grey-green tone, but the variegated form is greener, with a definite creamy pattern. The variegated nasturtium is an annual, but fortunately, does come true from seed. There was a variegated daisy – *Bellis perennis* (you have to get down on your hands and knees for this one) and a fabulous variegated Lamb's Ears, *Stachys lanata* 'Variegata'. This was not so much variegated, as having a medley of grey and green leaves interspersed with cream, giving a bold, cheerful effect.

A town garden in Talbot Street, Ellesmere.

The high, brick walls of the garden are, of course, perfect for climbers. One is a mass of Russian Vine – *Polygonum baldschuanicum* – wonderful with its great, airy, cream bunches of hanging flowers, individually tiny, but spectacular in the bunch. I must warn it's a terrible romper, you need a big wall for this one. The scent of honeysuckle fills the air, captured, and intensified by the walls.

The house is old, a timber framed building, constructed in 1690, forming the fourth wall of the garden. How an architecturally interesting house adds to the garden scene. A modern house, no matter how well designed, somehow never has the same ambience, or air of permanence. There is something so alluring about cultivating the same piece of land that others have toiled over for hundreds of years before. The longer the tenure, the greater the feeling of continuity.

Pink and red dianthus surround grey stone.

Here the house ties in well with the garden, the tiled area outside, being just the right size and scale.

There are many interesting ornaments scattered about, as well as a picturesque, round, open sided, summerhouse. The owner was fortunate in having the opportunity to purchase some good ornaments from a garden which was in the process of being broken up and sold. A graceful terracotta urn and base, came from a relation's house.

A large yew towards the end of the lawn makes life difficult in that part of the garden, the ground beneath being absolutely bone dry. The owner tries to choose plants which will accommodate dry shade, but it is an almost impossible task. Some well grown plants close by, but out of the yew's immediate influence, were a dark, raspberry-pink, sidalcea, and the very rare *Cosmos atrosanguineus*. The former is like a loose, pink delphinium, with extra large flowers. The latter, has single dahlia-like blooms, made out of the darkest, plum velvet-almost black. Also a para-hebe. I recently discovered this plant in my own garden, and, thanks to my visit to Talbot Street, was able to identify it. It trails along the ground, looking something like prostrate branches of *Eucalyptus gunnii*, with a blue flower at the end. They form dense mats of good ground cover, and are apparently quite hardy.

There is a shady, primrose lined path, to the rear garden, which is differentiated by a tall fence covered in white clematis, and various outbuildings. I noted *C.* 'Marie Boisselot' (the best big white) and 'Henryi', vigorous and free flowering, as well as my favourite rose, Climbing 'Cecile Brunner' – the perfect miniature button hole.

The rear garden is given over to propagation, vegetables and cutting borders. There is no front garden, the house fronting directly on to the road in true town style; though the garden can be reached from an alley, through a tall gate.

It's all too easy in this sort of small garden to overdo it. That is – more paving than plants, and that – just bought off the peg at Chelsea look. Somehow, both a country garden and country town atmosphere has been created here that is totally original. I can only say, that it suits both the owners and the house.

Upper Shelderton House ❀ Craven Arms

A large garden surrounding a modern house, set amidst the rolling, South Shropshire hills. Open under the N.G.S., see Yellow Book.

Upper Shelderton House garden reveals itself to the visitor as a series of pictures. Its charm lies in the gradual unveiling of each facet: the large, undulating lawn at the side of the house, leading you onwards to the woodland glade with azaleas and rhododendrons, the natural lake with its ring of mature trees, and the many well-filled island beds. It comes as a total surprise to learn that the whole garden was created in 1964.

The present occupants have lived with the garden for only five years. They have improved it considerably, but were fortunate to find a plot laid out by someone with such a good eye for design. The owner admits that it fulfilled almost untouched his ideal garden plan.

The soil is a neutral, sandy loam with an underlying strata of clay; though other top soil has been imported over the years, and I was astonished to hear that some not inconsiderable sized rocks were brought from Cumberland. These rock – now beautifully weathered – give one part of the garden a Japanese air. Adding to this theme is the water, a small stone bridge, and a huge stand of bamboo. The latter is cleverly planted where one can mow around it, thus restricting its growth.

The well thought out plan prevents the visitor from seeing all the garden at once, but with no perceptible barriers. Everything blends in the most natural way: one part of the garden leading into another with an absolute inevitability that denotes great self-confidence in the original design.

The island beds close to the house are filled with a mixture of plants both unusual and common. Among the latter were some real thugs – *Cerastium tomentosum*, Snow in Summer, and *Euphorbia cyparissias*, with short shaggy green stems and yellow bracts. Both dreadful runners, not to be planted carelessly, but looking wonderful at Upper Shelderton. The former with its grey leaves and white flowers drapes a low wall, which restricts its growth; the latter is in a bed which, like the bamboo, can be mown round.

All the outbuildings blend in well, probably because they are built of the natural, under-

Upper Shelderton House, wide lawns and well designed borders.

lying stones of the district. The swimming pool has a small garden to itself: the only way to deal with this difficult, modern addition to the garden scene.

Moving away from the house, the island beds change character: one full of heathers and dwarf conifers, another containing the Cumberland stone, carefully arranged to create a large, island rock garden.

Rock gardens are almost always a failure in small areas. The builders not having access to large enough stones to produce the necessary, natural picture, and falling into the trap of making a currants in a pudding (with the rocks laid on top of the soil) or dog's grave form – the latter speaking for itself. At Upper Shelderton House, the rocks are large and properly laid with an eye for the overall picture, the natural strata, and the lie of the land. The rockery has also been sympathetically planted with a pink weeping cherry, hosta, helianthemum, a delightful triple group of pointed conifers, softened by fluffy, bright-green, spring growth, and a carpet of Lily of the Valley.

Moving on to the woodland glade, all the loud rhododendrons and azaleas are toned down by the dark green background. This background and muted shade separates the bright hues and prevents the overpowering effect of so much colour. An outstanding rhododendron here is *R. campanulatum aeruginosum.* It had no flowers, but quite extraordinary metallic-blue new leaf growth, with a pale indumentum on the reverse, like nothing I have ever seen before. I suspect that you must catch it at its best in mid to late May for the full glorious effect.

Rhododendron campanulatum 'Aeruginsum'.

The large, natural pond has only one fault, it tends to become low in a hot, dry summer, exposing a muddy rim. Fortunately, the garden is big enough to cope with this disadvantage. The pond is surrounded by a mown walk and a diverse assortment of good trees. All our native deciduous kinds are represented, including a beautiful crateagus in full flower and a superb weeping copper beech. The conifers made a most satisfactory vertical contrast to the still, flat water.

This part of the garden is almost a conservation area, with butterflies and dragonflies on the dogwoods, plus a team of mallards enjoying themselves on the lake.

There are many interesting specimen trees on the wide lawn. Of particular note is a *Metasequoia glyptostroboides*, once though extinct and only rediscovered in China in 1947; also a large twisted willow, *Salix matsudana* 'Tortuosa', whose contorted branches are invaluable in flower arrangements, a variegated acer, *A. negundo* 'Variegatum', and a Silver-leaf Pear, *Pyrus salicifolia* 'Pendula', fronted by a reddish-pink berberis.

All in all, a near perfect garden, full of life and sparkle and providing a perfect setting for the house.

Walcot Hall Aboretum ✹ Bishops Castle

An architecturally distinguished house and thirty acre arboretum, planted by Lord Clive of India's son in 1800. Open under the N.G.S., see Yellow Book.

Walcot Hall is situated on rising ground, looking over surrounding wooded hills on the edge of the Clun Forest. It was purchased in 1764 by Lord Clive of India, though the house dates from earlier times. It was then largely redesigned by him into a typical, Georgian, country house of red brick, with a stable block and small village of dependants houses to match.

It was Lord Clive's son, however, who lived for many years in the house and planted the arboretum at the rear. The great trees are truly magnificent, but the mown, winding paths also lead past a variety of ornamental shrubs, especially fine rhododendrons and azaleas. These have been carefully planned to give colour throughout the year.

Huge trees and great expanses of water, Walcot Hall.

Many trees of the tallest or greatest girth in the county grow at Walcot, among them a Monkey Puzzle – *Araucaria Araucana*. Always a difficult tree to place, and so called because its stiff stems are impossible for a monkey to climb. I prefer to see this tree clothed down to the ground and not scarred by frost so that only a tuft of branches remains at the top, like some prehistoric feather duster.

There is also a huge Cedar of Lebanon – *Cedrus libani*, which has a crown spread of sixty feet, making it one of the county's biggest. An Atlas Cedar – *Cedrus atlantica* and a Deodar Cedar – *Cedrus deodara* are almost as large.

Other noteables are a Larch – *Larix decidua*, Eastern Hemlock – *Tsuga canadensis* (one of several giants) and a Douglas Fir – *Pseudotsuga menziesii*, described as one of the best in Britain. This is gardening on the largest scale, and certainly not to be attempted in a confined area.

Away from the arboretum, the beautiful parkland around the house contains many fine deciduous trees, including an avenue of beech leading up a rise towards the house, grazed uniformly level by persistent sheep.

The enormous, walled, kitchen garden now contains nothing but grass and an orchard of gnarled apple trees, its sinuous walls following the lie of the sloping land in undulating waves.

The woods full of great trees have a mystery all their own. As one wanders between the huge trunks, deep pools fringed by rushes and yellow iris reflect the far-away crowns, and bright rhododendrons light up dark corners like exotic torches. In medieval times this area around Lydbury North was the centre of the Royal Forest of Clun. Although it has largely been cleared away for farming, Shropshire is fortunate in retaining many trees, remnants of these great forests remaining in hedgerow and small copse.

As well as the arboretum, this classic English parkland of lakes, trees, and hills (including a view to the Longmynd as a backdrop) is second to none. Wild life abounds, much of the park being a bird sanctuary with hundreds of Canada Geese making their home on the lakes. There is also a small herd of Chinese water deer, though they are not often seen.

A sense of history pervades the whole area; not just because of an association with such an important historical figure as Clive of India, but reaching far back to a Hill Fort, reputedly from the time of Caractacus.

Nature and man have worked together at Walcot to produce a landscape of much variety and great beauty.

Wellington Road ❀ Donnington

Almost an acre of well planted garden, stocked with year around flower arranging in mind. **Not** *open to the public.*

This garden is an oasis of green peace and tranquility in the midst of the urban and suburban sprawl which surrounds Telford. Confined by a busy road, an army depot of low nissen huts, a railway line and a building site, it nevertheless manages to exorcize these horrors almost entirely by tall fences, good trees and clever planting.

The owner, who, as well as being a professional flower arranger, is a gardening correspondent working with Radio Shropshire, moved to Wellington Road in 1979. The site had been a rubbish tip, and boasted the grand total of two lilacs, two conifers and three pear trees. Less desirable were the broken bottles and the bed springs which littered the area. A J.C.B. removed fourteen skips of litter, and much top soil was imported.

It is a long, narrow garden, but the edges have been disguised with a screen of ash, elm and sorbus. The owner expects to lose the elms to Dutch Elm Disease every year, but so far has been lucky. I particularly admired a sorbus with extra large grey-green leaves called *S.* 'John Mitchell'. I believe it is a form of *S. cuspidata*, which varies greatly in the wild. This part of the garden houses a bed of very tall herbaceous

Alchemilla mollis fronts an urn and roses.

perennials, forming a background for a grey stone vase. They included a pale-yellow centaurea, rather like a scabious in size and shape, also *Macleaya cordata* with beautifully formed grey-brown leaves and tall, pale flowers. Both these are well over head height, and only to be attempted in the right place.

Every inch of the garden is utilized, with the ivies, 'Paddy's Pride', 'Gold Heart', and an intriguing variegated form of 'Cristata' I hadn't seen before, trained up trees. There were in fact many plants completely new to me in the garden, including a tree paeony with golden-brown, semi-double flowers described by the owner as 'beaten bronze'. *Hebe albicans*, with small, grey-green leaves and stubby white flowers nestled under the paeony. I had always assumed this was a dwarf form, but at Wellington Road it reached waist high. The soil, a neutral, sandy loam, must be good, as I also spied a well-grown choisya, though I realise that the recent mild winters have been much to these plants' liking.

One has to search for the treasures in this garden, I almost walked past a lovely clump of the variegated Solomon's Seal, *Polygonatum* × *hybridum* 'Variegatum'. Much more variegated than *P. falcatum* 'Variegatum', this is a tricky one to persuade to flourish. It rarely dies on you, but even worse, persists in looking unhappy. Having paid a small fortune for it, one is reluctant to throw it out. Seeing a well-grown plant gives one fresh heart to persevere. It obviously *can* be done. Further down the garden, I noted a pink form of *Rodgersia pinnata* (mine's white) probably *R.p.* 'Superba', as the colour was so good; also the delicate pink *Astrantia maxima*. All the astrantias are a delight, lasting well as a cut flower in water, but the latter is especially pleasing.

Wellington Road, Donnington.

The garden narrows even more at the end like the point of an arrow. Here the owner has created a shady area for many unusual ferns, including some rare crested varieties, plus hellebores, hostas, and a lovely white *Dicentra spectabilis*, 'Alba'. This part of the garden has nettles for butterflies, as well as being an over-wintering post for passing hedgehogs.

A round border in full sun, centred on a standard *Acer pseudoplatanus*

'Brilliantissimum' – whose early, shrimp-pink foliage is beloved by flower arrangers – contains a group of roses all named after characters in Shakespeare's plays. I find this a most intriguing idea. They include – 'Cressida', 'Pretty Jessica', 'Wise Portia', 'Moth', 'Fair Bianca', 'Lordly Oberon', and 'Proud Titania'. These are mostly the English Roses, raised by David Austin, a cross between the old shrub roses and modern varieties. They have the advantage of sweet scent and repeat flowering.

There is not a straight line in the whole garden, which disguises its oblong shape; though inevitably and logically, it consists of a long central lawn with wide borders on each side. Working our way back up towards the house, the foliage contrasts were lovely; the flower arranger coming to the fore for example in the extra good, blue-leaved, *Dicentra formosa* 'Langtrees', with purple-tipped, white flowers; also a yellow shaded lilac appropriately called 'Primrose'; *Heuchera cylindrica* 'Greenfinch', and the dark-leaved 'Palace Purple', as well as two strange roses.

The first, called 'Greensleeves', is pink in the bud, but gradually shades to green. The other – *Rosa sericea pteracantha*, boasts huge, flat, red, thorns, and delicate, ferny foliage like the pimpinellifolia roses.

Arriving at the small patio outside the house, I noticed some fine lilies, first by their heavy scent. These looked superficially like Regale, but were in fact a reverted form of Pink Perfection. They were held up by the glossy, dark green leaves of a *Camellia* 'Leonard Messel'. This the owner recommends as one of the very best, being both hardy and free-flowering in a strong, pink shade. Camellia foliage (if you can bear to cut it) is a good foil for lots of summer flowers; as are the hollies, mostly the non-prickly forms, which the owner grows for background in arrangements. *Prunus laurocerasus*, Common Laurel, with evergreen, dark-green, leathery leaves, fulfils the same purpose in my garden.

Wollerton Old Hall ❁ Hodnet

A one acre new garden set around an Elizabethan, cruck beam house and sympathetically designed in keeping with the period. Will be open under the N.G.S., in the future, see Yellow Book.

It must be unusual to have the opportunity to live as an adult in the house in which you were brought up as a child, especially if the house has passed out of the family hands in the meantime. The owner of Wollerton Old Hall was horrified at the deterioration of both house and garden since she lived there – the latter being little more than a field – but bought it anyway, and proceeded, with the assistance of her husband, successfully to renovate both.

It is an old sixteenth century black and white, timber framed house, but a young garden. I found it hard to believe that the owners had only been there five years. What they have accomplished in such a brief period, is little short of incredible. The next point that struck me, was how faithfully they had adhered to the period of the house in the general design of the garden. I think it unreasonable to confine the *plants* to those

115

available before the date of an old house in a private garden, as you miss so much. Very little remained of the original garden, except four good yews, which had to be seriously clipped back, and were then incorporated into the general design.

The owner remembers a brick knot garden close to the house, but all had disappeared, including – tragically – the hand made, brick pavers. This lost knot garden was remade in the same position as the old, using new, but good quality bricks, and box hedging (The owners grows all the box herself from cuttings). The design is Dutch, and this area is meant to be viewed from the upper windows of the house. It leads on to a sunken garden with round pond, gravel, and tubs. The retaining walls contain plants which like to lean over the edges, such as lavender and rosemary. There are urns filled with the pansy 'Raspberry Rose', beautifully placed seats facing each other across the pond, Swan River daisies, nicotiana, and *Cosmos* 'Purity' spilling out of the tubs. Vistas lead the eye in all directions: a lime alley heading down towards the main garden; a well-built, brick-pillared pergola, with a border of nepeta and climbing roses leads another way. I was strongly reminded of both Hidcote and Sissinghurst, by the garden within a garden concept, but the hedges are lower, allowing one glimpses of the whole from strategic points.

It is an immensely complicated plan, which was carefully worked out on paper. Much of the planting, however, is inspirational, using trial and error, which prevents the garden looking too regimented. The profuse planting also helps to soften the edges, and it will of course improve even more, as trees, shrubs and hedges reach maturity.

The owners had the advantage of a number of tall, well constructed, old walls, and have added to them in order to enclose the garden completely (this was the male half of the partnership's contribution). They prove the importance of getting the bones of the garden right first, in the shape of paths, gateways, etc. An iron gazebo which forms the

Part of the white and grey garden at Wollerton Old Hall.

centre piece to an intricate, white garden, has been several colours already in an effort to get it absolutely perfect. The owners admit a white and silver garden is something of a cliché nowadays; but a good idea is a good idea, how ever much it is used, and certainly looks wonderful at Wollerton. The paths are all narrow, crossing one another to form a pattern of squares. The gazebo covers a large pot of white agapanthus; and I also noted white foxgloves, Sea Holly, a white ceanothus and the white rose, 'Long John Silver', threaded with the sweetly scented Summer Jasmine. Most of the planting is kept low, however: white *Viola cornuta*, the filigree foliage of artemisia, Lamb's Ears and white lavender.

The boundary wall of the garden forms a superb backdrop for a spectacular herbaceous border, in full flower when we visited in late July. The colours ran from mauves, lavender, blues and pinks, through to white, orange, yellow, and harder reds. The plants encompassed – *Buddleia* 'Lochinch', delphiniums, penstemons, *Crambe cordifolia*, the Day Lily *Hemerocallis* 'Pink Damask', *Campanula lactiflora* 'Loddon Anna', *Geranium* 'Wargrave Pink' – to helichrysum, *Helenium* 'Coppelia', rudbeckia, ligularia, *Achillea* 'Gold Plate', phlox in every shade imaginable, and as many more. It is a visual tour de force, just the right amount of informality being introduced by self-sown *Verbascum bombyciferum* in the fronting gravel path. This tall, grey-flannel leaved plant, with soft, yellow flowers, is quite the best of the verbascums, and, although a biennial, once you have it, it will seed around.

The only curved lines in the garden come in a romatically, moody area with a small, deep green pond. There is a seat to contemplate it, a Kilmarnock willow, Asiatic primula, astilbe, lots of potentillas, and a Smoke Tree – *Cotinus coggygria* – in full flower. A border composed entirely of phlox, was doing well in the shade of an old sorbus, one of the few really big trees in the garden. Phlox are a particular favourite herbaceous perennial of the owner. They are certainly unbeatable for late flowers in a wide range of colours, but apparently prefer conditions somewhat damper than they have enjoyed in 1989.

Common plants are not despised in this garden. They are, of course, often common because they are good. That is, easy to grow, adaptable, and hardy. Rarity does not automatically confer distinction or desirability on plants. In fact, botanical elitism can often depress a garden, rather than lift it.

The garden ends in a brand new wall built with old brick. It has an undulating top, and is pierced by three openings – two solid wood doors and one central, wrought iron gate. There are plans to turn the small field beyond into a wild garden some time in the future. A new border of tender shrubs – abutilon and pittosporom for example – has been planted to utilize the protection offered. When all matures, it will be difficult to differentiate between the newly built walls and the originals, they have been so sympathetically incorporated into the pattern of the garden.

A long walk runs parallel

Wollerton Old Hall is noted for late summer colour.

with the wall, and it was interesting to see the soil held back by thin wooden strips; the ground ready and waiting for the next instalment of edging box to arrive from the greenhouse.

Making our way back to the house, we passed the wide, central axis, giving an uninterrupted view back to the top of the garden, past the lower borders and pleached lime avenue, over the two small gardens, sunken and knot, to the steeply gabled house.

The grass walk along the left side of the garden, begins with a group of old roses, skirts a small summerhouse, where we saw daunting pictures of the garden five years ago, and leads eventually to a pointed wooden gate, especially made to fit the wall. This brings you to the front of the house, passing a perfectly placed *Hydrangea sargentiana*, close to the wall, on the way.

There are saddle-stones and other ornaments, chosen to complement the house, set into the gravel. Larger trees, including a mulberry, hide surrounding buildings; though most are as picturesque as Wollerton Old Hall, and do not need to be disguised. With little to help them, other than a few good walls and a distant memory of past glories, the owners of Wollerton Old Hall have already made this garden one of the best in Shropshire. I am not exaggerating when I say, that, with maturity, it will be one of the best small gardens in the country.